A World of Change

EXPLORING OTHER CIVILISATIONS

Richard Tames

School of Oriental and African Studies,
University of London

Series editor: Rosemary Kelly

How to ……
The world in 1400 3
Henry the Navigator 5
Bartolomé de Las Casas 10
Leo Africanus 16
Matteo Ricci 22
William Adams 28
Captain John Smith 32
Jan Huyghen van Linschoten ... 40
Europe and the world
　in 1700 47
Find out more for yourself ... 50
Index 51

Nowadays we are slowly getting used to the idea that we are all living in 'one world'. Some people have called it a 'global village'. Others refer to it as 'spaceship earth'. What it means is that each part of the world depends on, and is affected by, others. Our daily news comes from around the world, and people like the Pope or the American President are famous not just in their own country but around the globe. In Europe we are used to eating Chinese or Indian style food and using cars made in Japan or electrical goods from Malaysia or sports goods from Korea. A rise or fall in the price of Middle Eastern oil, a good or bad harvest in Africa has a 'knock-on' effect on every other continent. A nuclear disaster in the Soviet Union threatens all the surrounding countries. But this situation is something very new in human history.

This book deals with how this first began to happen, and especially how people from very different countries began to come in contact with one another. You will see that this started a process by which people began to exchange not only goods but also plants, diseases and, most important of all, ideas. The results were to affect every aspect of human history from trade and war to technology and religion. The people who were caught up in this process each had their own dreams and desires. Perhaps they did not know that they were helping to make 'one world'. But they were.

Stanley Thornes (Publishers) Ltd

How to use this book

The great events which make up the theme of this book are presented to you through the specific experiences of real people who actually lived. This has the advantage of making them personal and vivid, rather than vague and abstract. But inevitably this approach raises problems as well. Not even the most tireless traveller can see everything. And each will have a particular interest and point of view. A missionary will probably be concerned to notice details of people's religions, just as a merchant will be especially knowledgeable about trade. So getting an overall picture will never be easy.

There is the problem of the sort of evidence they have left us. Henry the Navigator was a prince; and the lives and achievements of princes tend to be written by courtiers who often wish to flatter them and exaggerate their importance. Las Casas was a passionate champion of Indian rights, and deliberately presented a one-sided view of Spanish colonial rule because he believed it was so unjust and cruel. Leo Africanus left a marvellous account of his travels through Africa; but it is very difficult to check how accurate his reports were, just because he was one of the few who did write about this region. In other words, there is very little to check him against. And he was writing from memory in a place a long way away from the places and people he was describing, with no one nearby to check his memory of events. William Adams lived in Japan for twenty years, but all that survives of everything he wrote is just seven letters. John Smith wrote long and lively descriptions of America and the Indians; but we also know that he was much given to boasting. Can we believe what he says about his own part in the founding of the Virginia colony?

One major theme of this book is the building up of accurate geographical knowledge about the world. Maps are a very important source of evidence for this. Just compare any map drawn around the year 1400 with one from around 1700 and you will see a dramatic difference. But maps, too, present problems of evidence. Matteo Ricci found in China that educated people there had quite different ideas about the relative importance of the different countries in the world. The Portuguese treated maps of the route to the East as highly secret documents and prevented other nations from getting hold of them for more than a century. Linschoten's *Itinerario*, which finally gave the secret away, was a dramatic example of what would now be called commercial espionage.

Pictures present even more difficulties. Very few travellers were skilled artists. John White, who accompanied the English expedition to set up a colony on Roanoke Island, was a notable exception. His brilliant sketches and watercolours were eagerly copied by Dutch engravers. And their engravings were copied in turn by other printers who had never seen White's original material. So inaccuracies could easily creep in. Other printers were sometimes forced to rely entirely on written accounts of distant lands and peoples, without any way of checking their accuracy. And sometimes these accounts leave out important information. So one German picture of American Indians killing white settlers shows them doing so against a background of very German-looking houses, because the artist had no way of knowing what settler houses actually looked like, so he drew what he did know. So many of these pictures represent what Europeans thought foreign peoples and places *ought* to look like, rather than what they actually *did* look like.

And of course there are the women; or rather, there aren't. With rare exceptions, travel and trade were male activities, so women's points of view are often missing or must be guessed from evidence produced by men. By and large, the views of the peoples visited by the Europeans are likewise known only indirectly, through what the Europeans said about them. But despite all these problems, we must try to make as much sense of this tremendous story as we can. It is far too important to ignore, because it deals with the origins of the greatest problem of our own times – how different peoples can learn to live together in friendship on one small and fragile planet.

The world in 1400

This fourteenth-century French manuscript illustrates some of the very strange ideas that were held about the inhabitants of unknown lands. One of these imaginary people has his face on his chest, another has only one eye, and the third is shading himself with his single foot.

In 1400 the kings and peoples of Europe knew little of the world beyond its shores; and the kings and peoples of the rest of the world knew little of Europe. The difference between them was that the Europeans, or at least the more adventurous of them, were interested in doing something about it. They knew that to the East – though how far away they did not know – there were lands of immense power and wealth. From the East came spices and silks and jewels by long, dangerous and expensive overland routes. So the main purpose of the Europeans' so-called 'voyages of discovery' was not to discover new lands but new ways to reach old ones.

1 What methods of travel could Europeans use around 1400?

2 Why were silks, spices and jewels the main goods brought from the East?

Asians, by contrast, had little or no interest in Europe or the goods it produced. In their view, no European city could compare with the great cities of Asia. European languages sounded as strange as European clothes looked bizarre. Europeans came from the end of the world. Why should anyone take them seriously? Africans knew vaguely about Europe as a place from which the Moorish merchants of the Barbary (north Africa) coast brought fine swords and even finer horses. The peoples of America were completely ignorant of them.

3 Why do you think Asians were less interested in Europeans than Europeans were in Asians?

3

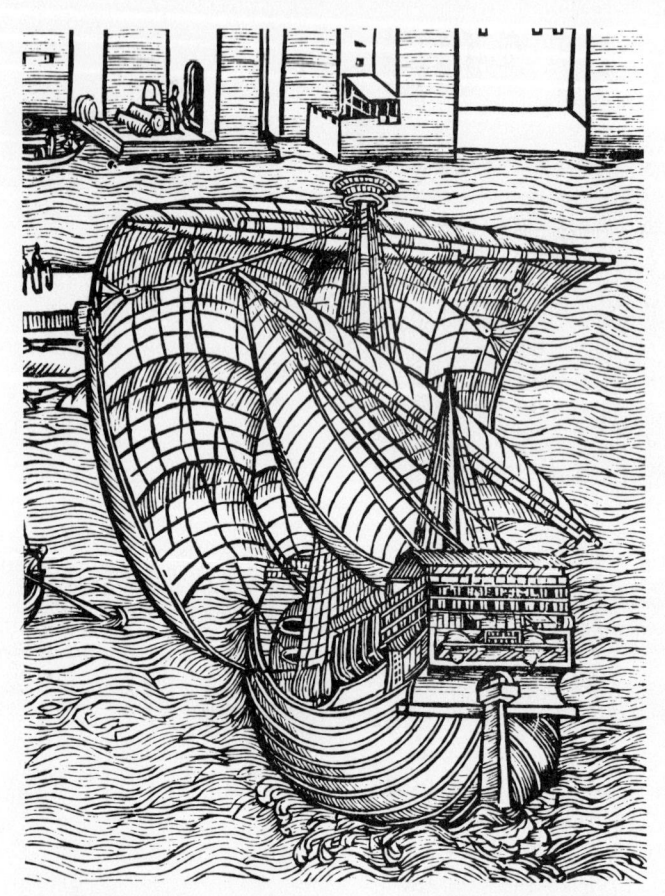

A common type of ship used by explorers. This wood-engraving is dated 1483.

An age of encounters

The main aim, and a main result, of European voyages was to make direct contact with the East; but there were many other and more important results. In looking for new routes to the East, European explorers found an ocean greater than the Atlantic and a continent as large as Europe and Africa put together. They discovered that the world was far, far bigger than any European had ever imagined. They found that there were other religions besides Christianity, Islam and Judaism; and they brought back to their own countries new plants, like potatoes and tomatoes, which became common European crops, as well as tea and tobacco, which became the objects of a great international trade. Above all, they proved that all the great oceans of the world were connected with one another and that the world was round.

1 Which was the ocean greater than the Atlantic?

2 Which was the continent larger than Europe and Africa put together?

3 Europeans believed many fantastic stories about faraway places. Some of the things they believed in, unicorns for example, we know did not exist. Make a list of things that *did* exist and which medieval Europeans might have found it difficult to believe in, such as elephants, coconuts, tobacco and tea.

4 Find out how the importation of tea on a large scale affected Britain, for example the effects on diet, fashion, the pottery industry and taxes.

5 Imagine you are a teacher in a European country in 1400. One of your pupils says that yours is the only important country in the world. What do you say?

6 Suppose a faraway country sent you only luxury goods. What would you be likely to think about that country?

Henry the Navigator

The edge of the world

The westernmost point of Britain is called Land's End. The westernmost point of Europe, in northwest Spain, is called Cape Finisterre. The name means the same; it comes from two Latin words *Finis* (End) and *Terra* (Land). A nobleman from Bohemia (now Czechoslovakia), called Leo of Rozmital, visited it around 1400 and found it to be a wild and barren place.

> One sees nothing anywhere but sky and water. They say that the water is so stormy that no one can cross it and no one knows what lies beyond. It is said that some tried to find out what was beyond,... but not one of them returned.

To the south of Cape Finisterre lies Portugal. Leo of Rozmital found the south a terrible place:

> One finds nothing to eat or drink for man or beast ... It often happens that no traveller is seen there for four or five years. The people ... go out very rarely, especially not at noon on account of the great heat ... They live mostly on fruit and drink no wine.

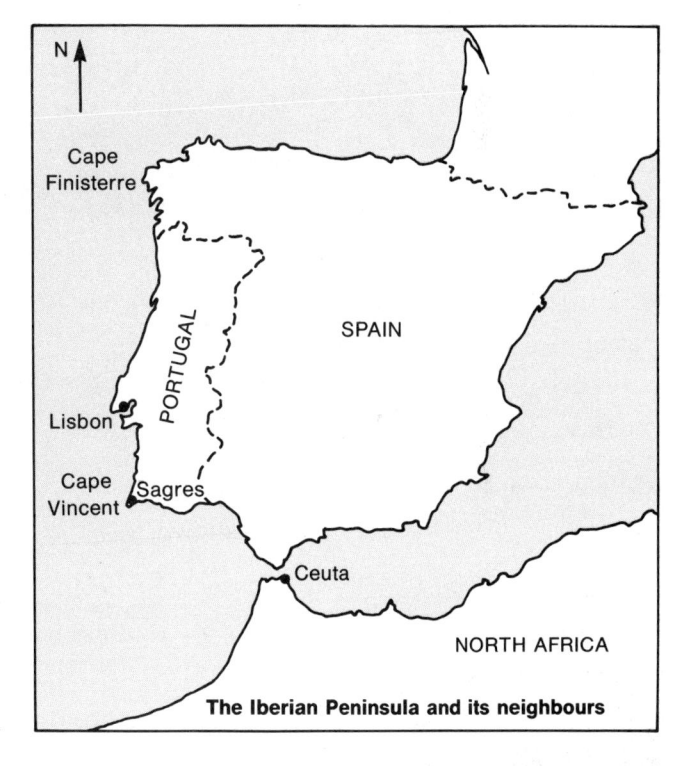

The Iberian Peninsula and its neighbours

Leo of Rozmital saw the weakness of Portugal, the poverty of its countryside. Its strength lay in the city of Lisbon, which had a fine harbour and grew rich on trade. In 1385 the wealthy merchants of Lisbon chose a new king and queen for Portugal, John of Avis and his English wife, Philippa of Lancaster. They had five sons. The third son, Henry, made Portugal the heart of an empire.

As a young man, Prince Henry of Portugal won fame in 1415 in an attack on the Moorish city of Ceuta in north Africa. Morocco was the farthest place he himself was ever to see, but he sent Europeans further into the

A panorama of Lisbon in the sixteenth century

unknown than they had ever been before. For this reason he has always been known to history as 'Henry the Navigator'.

■ The Portuguese were the first Europeans to send out ships to find new routes to the East? Why was it necessary for them to do this?

In Ceuta, Henry heard about the riches of Africa – ivory, gold and slaves – and decided to put Portugal in a position to reach them. When his father made him governor of the Algarve, Portugal's southernmost province, he went to live at Sagres on Cape Vincent, at the south-west tip of the country. Here he built a palace and Portugal's first astronomical observatory and gathered round him a team of experts on ship-building, map-making and seamanship. Henry did not discriminate on either religious or racial grounds. Some were, of course, Portuguese, but there were also Italians, Catalans (from eastern Spain) and even a Dane. Most were Christians, but some were Jews and Muslims.

Prince Henry the Navigator, 1394–1460

■ Why did Henry build an astronomical observatory?

Before Henry's time, European voyages into unknown seas had been haphazard and poorly planned. Henry made exploration a matter of state policy for the first time. Voyages would be made systematically and continuously, with clear objectives, by specially picked and trained men, backed up with the most up-to-date and detailed information available. From the harbour of Lagos, Henry sent out successive expeditions to search out the coast of west Africa, telling one of his captains:

> You cannot meet a danger so great that the hope of reward shall not be even greater.

■ Why do you think the ships Prince Henry sent out were more likely to be successful than the ones that had gone before?

Exploring West Africa

The first voyages led to the settlement of Madeira and the Azores, which had been reached more than fifty years earlier by sailors from Genoa in Italy. By making these islands permanent Portuguese territories, Henry not only gained profits from the production of timber, sugar and wine, but also established useful bases from which later expeditions could obtain supplies.

To the south of Morocco lay Cape Bojador (meaning 'outstretcher'), a low and sandy point feared for its currents and reefs. In 1434 one of Henry's ships rounded this point and returned safely. The next target was Cape Blanco, meaning 'White Cape', and so called because of its vast white beach. In 1441 one of Henry's captains returned to Portugal from this area bringing with him gold and prisoners. The prisoners were baptised as Christians and then sold as slaves. In 1448 a fort was established by the Portuguese on the island of Arguim, the first European settlement along the coast of Africa. Soon it became a major centre for the slave trade.

A caravel of the type used by the Portuguese

It was light and quick, and could sail in shallow water, helping the Portuguese greatly in their voyages of exploration.

■ Why do you think the captives were baptised?

By the time Henry died in 1460, his captains had explored 1,500 miles of the west African coast and reached the River Gambia. Henry had made money from his control of business in tuna fish, sugar and soap and from the new trades in gold and slaves, but he ploughed it all back into new expeditions and died in debt.

A route to the East

Henry's nephew, John II of Portugal (reigned 1481-95) continued his work and, because he was King, was able to put much more money into it. In 1487 he sent Bartolomeo Dias on a voyage which took him right round the southernmost tip of Africa. Dias was in fact blown round and so he called the place the Cape of Storms. John realised that a sea route to the East was now possible, so he renamed it the Cape of Good Hope.

When a Genoese seaman called Cristobal Colon (Christopher Columbus) asked John to provide the money for an expedition to sail west in the hope of finding a new route to India, John turned down his request. Dias had already given him a route to India by going eastwards, and between 1497 and 1499 Vasco da Gama had proved that John had been right, by sailing all the way to India via the Cape of Good Hope, and back again.

■ Why do you think the discovery of a sea route to the East was so important?

John's successor, Manuel the Fortunate (reigned 1495-1521), saw Lisbon grow even richer on the new African trade. Woollen cloth from England and metals from Germany were traded for pepper and slaves from Africa. Some of the new wealth went to build a fabulous monastery at Belem, near Lisbon, elaborately decorated with carvings of waves and sea-shells, ropes and ships, and leaves and fruits from tropical lands.

■ The King of France called the King of Portugal 'Manuel the Grocer'. Why do you think this name was chosen?

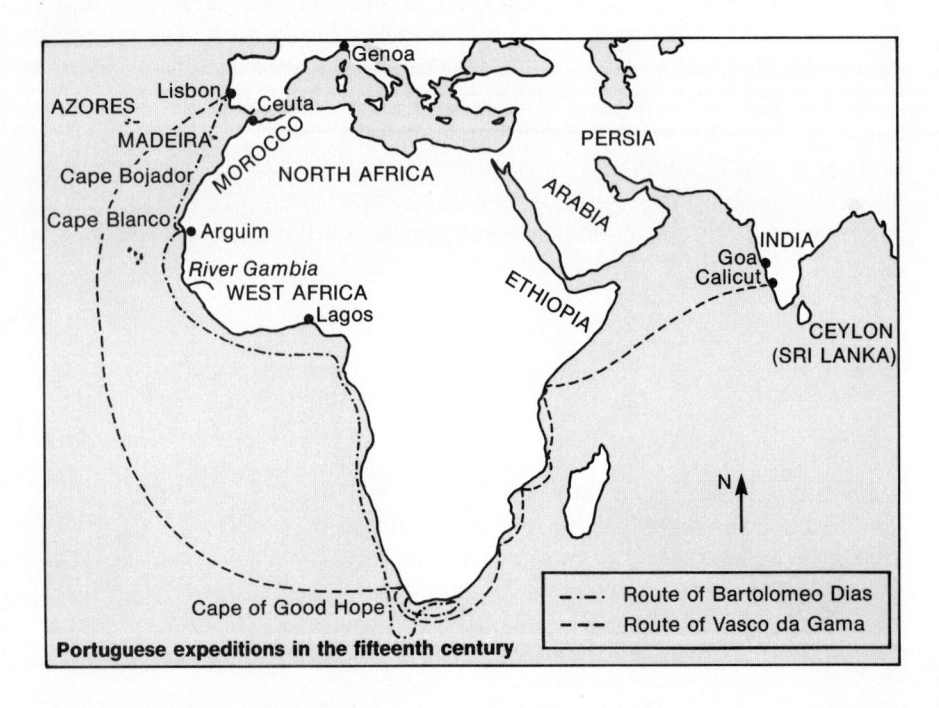

Portuguese expeditions in the fifteenth century

In 1499 Manuel claimed a Portuguese monopoly of 'the conquest, navigation and commerce of Ethiopia, Arabia, Persia (modern Iran) and India'. In 1510 they were able to set up a permanent trading station or 'factory' at Goa on the western coast of India; this was the first European settlement in Asia. They then moved on to China (see page 22).

Triumph or disaster?

Portuguese exploration was celebrated in a great poem, *The Lusiads*, by the soldier–poet Luis de Camoes (pronounced Camoynsh) (1524–80). Here is the beginning of his poem translated into English:

> This is the story of heroes, who leaving their native Portugal behind them opened a way to *Ceylon* and further, across seas no man had ever sailed before. They were not ordinary men, at home in war and every kind of danger; they founded a new kingdom among distant peoples, and made it great. It is the story too of a line of kings who pushed forward the frontiers of faith and empire, spreading confusion among the unbelievers of Asia and Africa and achieving immortality through their famous deeds. If my talent proves equal to the task, all men shall know of them.

modern Sri Lanka

■ Why do you think the Portuguese now think of Camoes as a national hero?

However, in 1608 another Portuguese writer wondered whether it had all been worthwhile:

> The price of the brilliant discoveries, the bravery and endurance, was that as we went forward in the discovery of the world, farming in Portugal grew worse ... all this wealth from the conquests in India, which brought to Lisbon parrots in golden cages, gave us no fields in which to sow crops or graze cattle, or men to work those fields. On the contrary, it took away men who might have done this work ... I do not put much faith in Indian things. Men should keep busy with what they have at home.

1 Do you agree with what this writer says about the Portuguese expeditions, especially his last statement?

2 Were voyages of exploration just a matter of making countries richer?

3 During these voyages of exploration, the Portuguese language spread to many countries. Try to find out in which countries Portuguese is still spoken today.

4 Imagine you are a Portuguese writer or poet. Write a passage or poem in praise of Henry the Navigator, then illustrate your work, using ideas taken from this chapter.

5 Design a mural for a wall at Belem monastery; or draw a fifteenth-century sailing boat, based on the illustrations on pages 4 or 7, or on any other illustration you can find.

Bartolomé de Las Casas

A sixteenth-century map showing South America

Conquistadors and kings

The Spanish conquest of South America was the work of *conquistadors*, rough, tough soldiers of fortune. They had gone, they said, 'for God and for gold'; but mostly they had gone for gold. They overthrew the great empires of the Aztecs in Mexico and the Incas in Peru and then looked forward to a life of ease and plenty, while the defeated Indians worked the lands and the mines that would keep them wealthy. The conquistadors had left Spain on their own initiative and at their own expense. The kings of Spain had given them little assistance except official blessings. But as the conquest was completed the Crown began to claim the right to rule these distant lands as its own. There were a number of reasons for this:

1. The kings of Spain had driven out the Muslim Moors and crushed the power of great feudal barons. In their own land of Spain they stood supreme. They were not likely to let this powerful new military aristocracy come to power in new Spanish-speaking lands abroad.
2. The 'New World' was rich in gold and silver. The Spanish Crown could use this wealth to strengthen itself against rival nations in Europe.
3. It was the duty of a Christian ruler to spread the faith. The King of Spain had been given a special title by the Pope – 'His Most Catholic Majesty' – and he therefore had a special responsibility to do so.

■ How do you think the conquistadors would react to the Spanish kings' claim to rule the New World?

Ruling an empire faced the Spanish throne with some important questions: Was it right to convert Indians to Christianity by force? Was it right to make Indians slaves? Should Indians have the right to the protection of law, like other Spanish subjects?

■ What do you understand by the term 'slave'? Can slaves have rights? How could being a Christian make a difference to a slave?

A note on 'Indians'
When European explorers sailed west, they were looking for the spices and gems of 'the Indies'. By the time they realised they had found something different – an entirely new continent – they had become used to calling all the inhabitants of this 'New World' Indians, and they went on doing so. The name was quite wrong, of course, and it described what were really many different peoples.

This sixteenth century woodcut gives an imaginary view of the native peoples of the New World welcoming Columbus. Notice the soldiers on the left putting up the cross.

'Natural slaves'?

The Spanish colonists living in South America argued that the Indians were idle and vicious savages who could only be tamed gradually and civilised by forced labour on plantations and mines. They wanted the Spanish Crown to interfere as little as possible on behalf of the Indians. The colonists obviously wanted to look after their own interests; and they found an ally in Juan Gines de Sepulveda (1490–1573), who based his arguments on the ideas of the ancient Greek philosopher, Aristotle. Aristotle had said that in nature it was right for 'higher' forms of life to have power over 'lower' ones. So there was a 'natural' authority of adults over children, humans over animals, and so on. Sepulveda argued that Indians – all Indians – were entirely inferior to Spaniards – all Spaniards. Their inferiority was proved, he argued, by the fact that some of their customs were barbaric, for example human sacrifice and cannibalism, and because they could not reason or be expected to behave like civilised men. At best, they were like wicked children, over whom the Spanish should have a father's authority.

A friar 'teaching' Christianity

1 Why did some people think that slavery was right in the sixteenth century?

2 Why do most people nowadays agree that it is wrong?

Bartolomé de Las Casas

Las Casas

A very different point of view was held by Bartolomé de Las Casas (1474–1566). He was the son of a Spanish merchant and was brought up in Seville, the great port which grew rich on Spain's trade with the New World. In 1502 he went to the island of Hispaniola to help its new Spanish governor spread Christianity among the local Indian population. After a decade of first-hand experience he was convinced that forced labour was harmful rather than beneficial to the Indians. In 1514 he gave up his rights over the land and Indians allotted to him and in 1515 returned to Spain to plead for a change in government policy. For the next fifty years he was to be the most ardent champion of the Indian cause.

■ Why do you think Las Casas became an influential person on the question of Indian rights?

In 1520 Las Casas returned to South America with a team of officials to investigate Indian conditions and report back to the government. But he was deeply disappointed with the rather half-hearted measures that the team recommended, so he decided to develop a practical alternative instead. The Crown granted him a piece of land in Cumana (now part of Venezuela) to be colonised without conquest. Here he set up towns of 'free' Indians. But the attempt ended in failure when the Indians rose in revolt in 1521. They had been badly treated by Spaniards in the past and were not prepared to trust any of them again. Las Casas fled to the monastery of Santo Domingo, where he joined the Dominican order of friars and spent twelve years working on his massive book called *History of the Indies*.

■ Why do you think Las Casas decided to write a history book?

In 1535 Las Casas was sent to Peru by his superiors in the Dominican order. On the way his ship was forced by a storm to break its journey in Nicaragua, where he criticised local Spanish treatment of the Indians so strongly that he was forced to flee to Guatemala. Here, he tried to convert the Indians peacefully, without using force, but the Indians were still mistrustful of him, and he had little success. He later wrote about his experiences in a book called *The Only Method of Attracting All People to the True Faith*. Returning to Spain in 1540, Las Casas wrote *A Very Brief Account of the Destruction of the Indies,* which described the cruelties of the Spanish colonists and led King Philip II to introduce a code of 'New Laws', which abolished Indian slavery and greatly limited the rights of the colonists over the Indians. The 'New Laws' provoked a violent reaction in America and were quickly changed, though they did serve to warn the colonists that there were some limits on the way they could treat the Indians.

Las Casas went back to the New World as Bishop of Chiapas (now part of Guatemala) but again made himself so unpopular by criticising local Spanish rule that he was forced to return to Spain in 1547. He spent the rest of his life completing his *History of the Indies* and criticising the government's colonial policy, which always seemed to him to be out of touch with the actual situation.

An Indian is maltreated by a Spaniard and forced to transport his goods.

A great debate

In 1550 Las Casas had the chance to debate the Indian question face to face with his opponent, Sepulveda. Appearing at the request of the Crown at Valladolid, in Spain, both sides set out their arguments. Las Casas rejected Sepulveda's argument that a whole people could be 'natural slaves'. At worst, he suggested, a few wicked or backward individuals might be. Las Casas upheld the duty of the Spanish Crown to convert the Indians

A battle between Indians and Spaniards

to Christianity. The conquistadors had taken priests with them and tried to force Christianity on the Indians. Las Casas warned that force would make conversion more, rather than less, difficult. Therefore peaceful methods had to be used:

non-Christians

> The *infidels* ... (who by nature are very gentle, humble and peaceful) should be persuaded by gifts and presents, and nothing should be taken away from them. And thus they will regard the God of the Christians as a good, gentle and just God. Hence they will want to be His subjects and to receive His Catholic faith.

Indeed, Las Casas argued, the authority of the Spanish Crown rested on its duty of peaceful conversion and protecting the basic rights of the Indians as human beings:

Spain

> The kings of *Castile* are obliged by divine law to establish a government and administration over the native peoples of the Indies that will preserve their just laws and good customs and abolish the evil ones which are very few ... whatever faults their society may have had can be removed and corrected with the preaching and the spread of the gospel.

On balance the arguments of Las Casas won the day. But although the Spanish Crown inclined to greater control over American affairs, most Spanish nobles saw more advantage to themselves and their relatives if royal control remained weak. Las Casas still argued that the Crown had an obligation to fulfill. Indeed it had years of neglect to make up for.

■ What evidence is there that the Spanish Crown was very concerned about the Indian question?

A civilising mission

The Spanish conquistadors claimed to be bringing Christianity and civilisation to the Indians. Looking back on the first half-century of Spanish rule, Las Casas saw little but cruelty and exploitation:

payments or gifts

> The Indians were prevented from receiving the Christian faith ... The wretched and tyrannical Spanish worked the Indians night and day ... They collected unbelievable *tributes* ... forced the Indians to carry burdens on their backs ... as if they were less than beasts. They persecuted and expelled from the Indian villages the preachers of the faith ... And I solemnly affirm, as God is my witness ... all the authority of the Kings, even if they were resident in the Indies, will not be enough to prevent all the Indians from perishing.

1 Why do you think the Spanish colonists tried to stop preachers spreading the Christian faith among the Indians?

2 Why do you think it might have made a difference if the Spanish kings had lived in the New World?

This nineteenth-century copy from a sixteenth-century Mexican manuscript shows Aztec nobles paying tribute to a Spaniard.

The kings were never resident in the Indies and, although they tried to make laws which would protect the Indians from cruel treatment, it was difficult to enforce them at so great a distance. Forced labour and new diseases from Europe, such as smallpox, killed millions of Indians, and it took several centuries for most of them to become even second-class citizens in their own lands. But they did not perish entirely, as Las Casas had feared. And for that the Catholic Church can take much of the credit. The King of Spain was far away, but the Church was not. In Las Casas the Church found a man whose voice could not be ignored. It followed his example in supporting and protecting the Indians. Repeated failure never defeated him and both the example of his life and his many writings made sure that the message of this 'Apostle of the Indies' would never be forgotten.

1 Do you think Las Casas was a success or a failure?

2 Which South American countries are Catholic nowadays? Use your school library to do some research into this.

3 Find out which South American countries still have large Indian populations.

4 a) Imagine you are an Indian captured by the conquistadors and subjected to slavery. Make notes on your feelings towards the conquistadors.

Or

b) Imagine you are an Indian working in Cumana under Bartolomé de Las Casas. Make notes on your feelings towards him.

If you wish, you may accompany your notes with illustrations.

5 Find out as much as you can about William Wilberforce. What did he have in common with Las Casas?

Leo Africanus

A sixteenth-century map of the coast of North Africa

An interrupted journey

In the year 1518 an Arab galley was sailing past the island of Djerba, just off the coast of Tunisia. On board was a young man called al-Hassan ibn Muhammad al-Wazzani. He would probably have asked his fellow-passengers to call him al-Fasi, the man from Fez. The city of Fez in Morocco was famed for its great university. Anyone who spoke to the young man would soon have guessed from his speech that he was well-educated, and this would have been confirmed by the fact that he was probably clutching a large bundle of notes in Arabic, the first draft of a book which was to describe his wonderful travels in Africa. After several years of wandering and adventures the young man was at last on his way home to complete his book in comfort.

But he never got there. Before the ship could reach the shore it was captured by Christian pirates and all the passengers and crew were either killed or taken prisoner. Usually captives were sold at the great slave markets in the Italian cities of Genoa and Pisa, but even the pirates were impressed by the young Muslim scholar, who soon proved that he could speak Spanish as well as fluent Arabic. So they decided to send him to Rome, as a present for Pope Leo X.

■ Why did it help so much that he could speak Spanish?

Leo X was the son of Lorenzo the Magnificent, the prince whose generous patronage of artists and men of learning had made Florence Italy's most brilliant city. The Pope followed his father's example and filled his court with scholars, artists and craftsmen. After he had interviewed the young Arab captive he immediately set him free, baptised him as a Christian and gave him the same names as himself, in Italian Giovanni Leone; but he is known to history by his Latin name, Leo Africanus, Leo the African.

■ Why do you think the Pope and his father gave so much money to pay for scholars and artists?

Leo's great book

The Pope gave Leo money to live on and ordered him to finish his book. It took him until 1526, three years after the Pope himself had died, and it was not published in printed form until 1550. Many years later it was translated into English and then published in London in 1600 as *The History and Description of Africa and the Notable Things therein contained*. For almost another two hundred years it was to remain Europe's most important source of information about the interior of Africa. Map-makers and merchants relied on it for facts; but the book also spread the idea generally among Europeans that Africa was a continent of immense wealth and terrifying dangers. The translator of Leo's book wrote:

> Moreover, as touching his exceeding great Travels – I marvel much however he should have escaped so many thousands of imminent dangers... How often was he in hazard to have been captived, or to have had his throat cut by the prowling Arabians and wild Moors? And how hardly many times escaped he the Lion's greedy mouth, and the devouring jaws of the Crocodile?

■ Why do you think it took so long for Leo's book to be printed and translated?

A man of talent

Apart from his famous book, little is known of Leo's life and personality, though we can easily guess that he must have been tough and resourceful, as well as clever. He was born in the beautiful mountain city of Granada in southern Spain in 1493 or 1494, on the eve of its capture by the Christians. His father was a man of wealth who was able to take his family to a comfortable exile in north Africa, where they settled in Fez, a city as renowned for trade as for learning. As an Arab, Leo of course spoke Arabic as his first language. But he also learned Spanish which would be very useful if his family should ever return to Spain from exile in Africa. In Fez, Leo proved himself to be an outstandingly able pupil, who soon qualified as a lawyer and turned his hand to one occupation after another – clerk, judge, diplomat, poet and merchant. He travelled not only up and down

Pope Leo X

the entire coast of north Africa, but as far away as Constantinople (now Istanbul) and across the Black Sea to the Crimea. But it was the interior of Africa which drew him most strongly.

1 Why do you think Leo must have been tough and resourceful as well as clever?

2 How did his background fit him to become a travel writer?

The golden trade

In the early sixteenth century the coastal cities of north Africa specialised in trade with each other and with the Christian ports of the Mediterranean. The trans-Saharan trade with the interior of Africa was controlled by a string of inland cities – Fez, Sijilmasa, Tlemcen, Wargla and Ghadames. Through these cities passed the goods most wanted by the Africans of that vast area which geographers called the Sudan, a territory stretching from present-day Mali to modern-day Sudan. What the Africans most wanted was European cloth, sugar, brass pots, books and fine horses, and they paid for them with slaves, gold and animal hides. Where the paths were too rough for camels the Africans used slaves to carry their wares to and from the trading stations.

■ What problems were there in trading across the Sahara?

Leo was determined to see the land of slaves and gold for himself, and he did so twice. The first time was around 1510, when he had just left school. He accompanied his uncle on a diplomatic mission from the Sharif, or ruler, of Fez to Askia Muhammad Ture, the warrior founder of the great empire of Songhay. Three years later, travelling as a merchant, Leo re-visited the lands of this ruthless but splendid ruler. His writings therefore give us not only descriptions of the landscape, cities and peoples of the Sudan but also an account of one of its most powerful states at the height of its greatness.

■ How do you think it might have helped Leo to make two journeys into Africa rather than just one?

Timbuktu

Leo's first journey began with a crossing of the Atlas mountains to Sijilmasa and then on into the desert, where there were constant threats from prowling nomads. Leo and his uncle were very glad to reach Walata, the most northerly city of Songhay, where they received a friendly welcome. Then they went on to Timbuktu, one of the new empire's provincial capitals, with a population of some 25,000 people. Leo did not think much of their houses, which he described as 'cottages built of chalk and covered with thatch'; but he was impressed by 'a most stately temple...and a princely palace also built by a most excellent workman of Granada'. And even if the people were not housed very well, their way of life was certainly pleasant enough:

> Here are many wells containing most sweet water; and whenever the river Niger overflows they convey its waters by certain sluices into the town. Corn, cattle, milk and butter this region yields in great abundance; but salt is very scarce here, for it is brought by land from Taghaza, which is 500 miles distant ... The inhabitants are people of a gentle and cheerful disposition, and spend a great part of the night in singing and dancing through all the streets of the city.

But Leo and his uncle had not come to see the common people. They had come to meet the governor of the city:

> The rich *king* of Timbuktu has many plates and sceptres of gold ... When he travels anywhere he rides on a camel which is led by some of his noblemen ... Whosoever will speak to this king must first fall down before his feet, and then taking up earth must sprinkle it upon his own head and shoulders ... He always has 3,000 horsemen and a great number of footmen that shoot poisoned arrows, attending upon him. They often have skirmishes with those that refuse to pay tribute and so many as they take they sell to the merchants of Timbuktu. Here are very few horses bred ... but their best horses are brought out of Barbary.

king — governor

■ Why do you think horses were valued so much?

Leo was also clearly impressed by the fact that the governor of Timbuktu was not only wealthy and powerful, but also cultured:

> Here are great store of doctors, judges, priests and other learned men, that are bountifully maintained at the king's cost and charges. And hither are brought *divers* manuscripts or written books out of Barbary, which are sold for more money than any other merchandise.

divers — various

■ Why do you think Leo particularly approved of the governor's generosity to men of learning?

Leo saw Timbuktu at its best and was no doubt very surprised to come across a flourishing city in the middle of an immense desert. But his enthusiastic account of it misled his readers into thinking it a far more magnificent place than it in fact was. When the traveller, Réné Caillie, went there three centuries later he was bitterly disappointed:

> I had formed a totally different idea of the grandeur and wealth of Timbuktu. The city presented, at first view, nothing but a mass of ill-looking houses, built of earth.

■ Do you think Caillie was reasonable to think Timbuktu might still be the same as it had been three hundred years before?

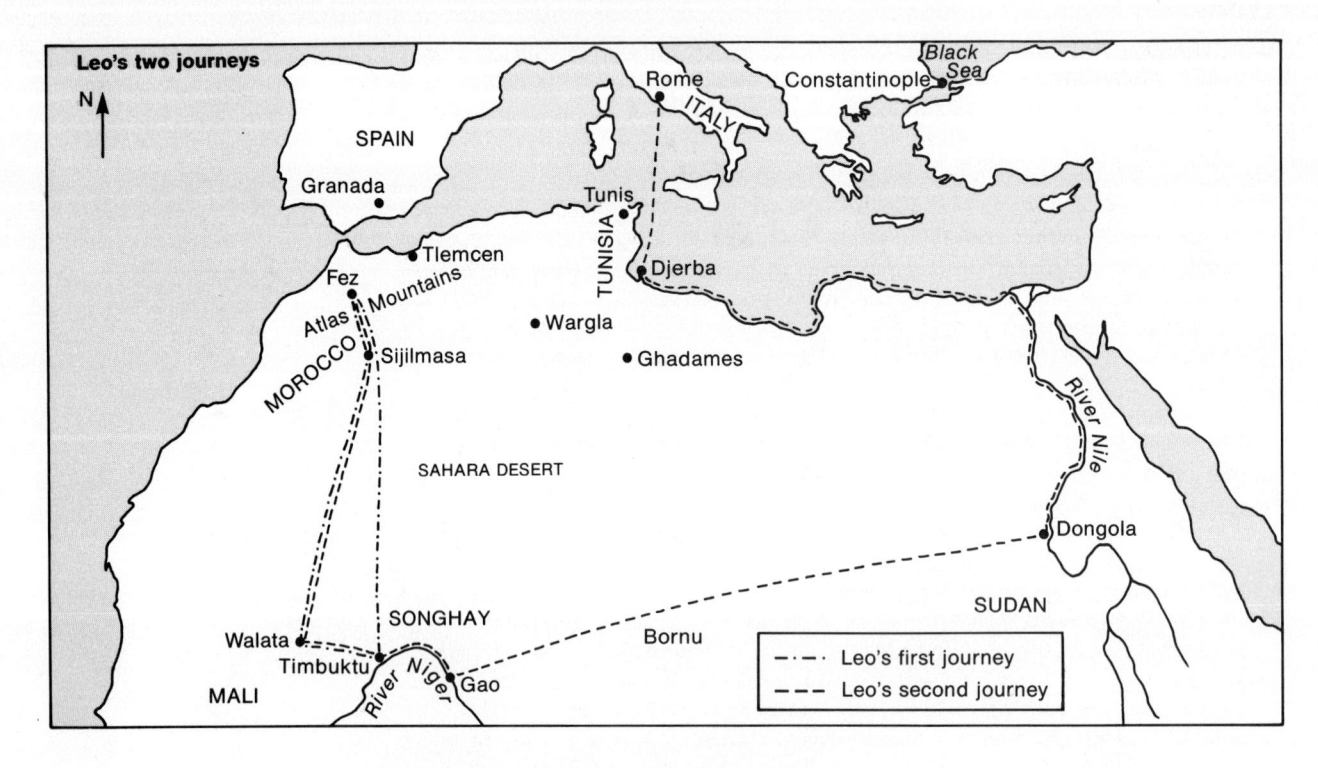

Leo's second journey

On this first visit to the Sudan, Leo appears to have returned directly from Timbuktu to Morocco. But his second trip took him back along the same route and then on to Gao, the Songhay capital. Again, he thought the houses of the people 'mean', or humble, but was astonished at the commerce of the city:

golden coins

golden coins

> It is a wonder to see what plenty of merchandise is daily brought hither and how costly and sumptuous all things be. Horses bought in Europe for ten *ducats* are sold again for 40 ... There is not any cloth of Europe so coarse, which will not be sold here ... A sword here is valued at 3 or 4 *crowns* and so likewise are spurs, bridles ... and spices also are sold at a high rate; but of all other commodities salt is most extremely dear.

1 Why do you think the prices of European goods were so high?

2 Why was salt so expensive?

Continuing his journey through the Songhay empire Leo saw many places which had once been independent kingdoms but had been devastated by Askia's armies or crushed by the taxes he took from them. Leaving Songhay, Leo passed through Bornu, where even the king's dogs wore chains of gold, and where horses were so prized that a single mount could be exchanged for 15 or 20 slaves. Fast, strong horses were invaluable when the king of Bornu went raiding for slaves and treasure.

Leo's eastward journey ended at Dongola on the Nile. From there he followed the river north to the coast of Egypt and then he went, not to Morocco as he had intended, but to his unexpected exile in Rome, after his capture by Christian pirates in 1518. Leo's stay in Europe was not to be a permanent one. Eventually he went back to his own people, settling in Tunis, and reverted to his former religion, Islam. He died around 1552 renowned for many years to come as Europe's leading expert on the wonders of unknown Africa.

1 Why do you think Leo's book remained important for so long?

2 Name the main qualities and abilities which made Leo Africanus such an outstanding explorer; then list any faults that you think he had.

3 Design a sixteenth-century travel brochure tempting tourists to north and west Africa. What sort of people would have enjoyed travelling there?

Timbuktu in the seventeenth century

Leo's great mistake

For centuries the ancient Greek writer Herodotus (484–425 BC) was regarded by Europeans as the authority on geography. He wrote that just as Europe was divided by the Danube, flowing from west to east, so Africa was also divided by a great river flowing in the same direction. In the tenth century Ibn Haukal, the first Arab geographer to visit the Sudan, confirmed that the Niger did indeed flow east. In contradiction, two centuries later, al-Idrisi, the most influential of all Arab geographers said that the Niger flowed west, although he had never actually seen it himself. And he was still believed even after the fourteenth century traveller Ibn Battuta, who had seen it, confirmed that the Niger did in fact flow east. Leo had the chance to settle the matter, but this is what he wrote:

> The river Niger passes through the middle of the country of the blacks... Some people say that the river rises in the mountains in the west and flows eastward to form a lake. This is not *exact*; we ourselves have navigated the river from Timbuktu... and followed the current to the kingdoms of Jenne and Mali, both of which lie to the west.

correct

Nobody knows for certain how Leo made such a basic mistake. Perhaps his memory was at fault, or perhaps scholars in Rome persuaded him into believing he was mistaken. Find the River Niger in a modern atlas and see if you can discover how Leo has made his mistake. Whatever the reason, European map-makers continued to show the Niger flowing west until the Scottish explorer, Mungo Park, finally settled the matter in 1796, when he saw with his own eyes that it did in fact flow east.

Matteo Ricci

A seventeenth-century map of China

The celestial empire

Five hundred years ago China was one of the most powerful countries in the world. It had more people than all the kingdoms of Europe added together, and those people were probably better governed. Certainly the Chinese thought so. The Chinese thought of themselves as the most civilised people on earth and of their government as 'The Celestial (Heavenly) Empire'. Neighbouring peoples, like the Koreans and Japanese, were regarded as civilised just so far as they copied Chinese laws and customs. Other peoples were simply looked down on as 'barbarians'.

1 The Chinese called their country 'Chung Kuo', which means 'The Central Kingdom'. Why do you think they chose this name? What does it tell you about their attitude to other peoples?

2 Why do you think the Koreans and Japanese did copy some Chinese laws and customs?

The coming of the barbarians

In 1516 a Portuguese merchant ship reached Canton, the great port of southern China. On board this ship were some Portuguese ambassadors on their way to Peking, the Chinese capital. They were hoping to visit the emperor; but when they arrived, they were turned away by Chinese officials.

■ Why do you think the Portuguese wanted to see the emperor, and why were they turned away?

The Portuguese gradually established trading posts from India to Japan, which they reached in 1543. In 1557 they established a trading station at Macau, a small peninsula near Canton. The Chinese allowed them to trade provided they stayed there and carried out all their business through Canton. In 1575 the first Catholic missionaries reached Canton. Seven years later Matteo Ricci came to join them. He was to stay in China until his death in 1610.

The wise man from the West

Matteo Ricci became known among the Chinese as 'The Wise Man from the West', although it took a long time for him to earn their respect. He was a highly educated man, and an expert on mathematics and astronomy in particular. When he arrived in China he set out to become an expert on the Chinese, their language, their customs and their methods of government. He had come to teach them about Christianity, but he recognised that they were a proud people, sure of their own ideas and suspicious of foreigners. He realised that he would have to be very patient and explain things in the ways that the Chinese would think of as reasonable. Even his appearance was against him, because he had blue eyes and a curly beard.

■ Why do you think Ricci's appearance mattered?

China and its neighbours

After a number of delays Ricci was allowed to set up a permanent mission on the West River near Canton. He thought that the most important people to influence were the mandarins, the learned officials who ruled China on behalf of the emperor; and he thought that the best way to do that was to show them some of the new achievements of western science, rather than to try to tell them about religion straightaway. So he entertained them at his house, talked to them politely in Chinese and showed them his collection of clocks, globes and astronomical instruments. The mandarins were really quite interested. One of them wrote:

> He is very polite when he talks to people and his arguments if challenged, are without end. Therefore, even in foreign countries, there are gentlemen.

■ Why did Ricci decide to try to influence the mandarins first? Do you think his approach was likely to be successful?

Through Chinese eyes

When Ricci showed his mandarin friends a western map of the world some of them laughed, and others were angry. All Chinese thought that China was at the centre of the world. Father Trigault, who translated Ricci's diaries, explained what happened:

> They did not like the idea of our geographies pushing their China into one corner... They could not understand... that the earth is a globe, made up of land and water, and that a globe, by its very nature, has neither beginning nor end.

So Ricci drew a new version of his map:

> He left a margin on either side of the map, making the Kingdom of China appear right in the centre. This was more in keeping with their ideas and gave them a great deal of pleasure and satisfaction.

The mandarins began to take Ricci seriously:

> Seeing the names of many places in perfect accord with those given by their own ancient writers, they admitted that the chart really did represent the size and figure of the world. From that time on they had a much higher opinion of the European system of education.

Ricci's re-drawn map was engraved and printed, and used throughout China.

■ What do you think of Ricci's approach to this problem?

A mandarin sitting as a judge

Note the instruments of torture on the floor.

Peking

In 1589 disorder in Canton led Ricci to move north towards the capital, but it was not until 1600 that he was able to reach Peking itself. (Remember that he was a foreigner in a strange country and had to settle wherever he could find friends and peace.) The emperor had finally heard about him and invited him to present himself at court.

1 Why do you think Ricci wanted to go to Peking?

2 Why do you think the emperor had taken so long to hear about Ricci?

At court Ricci was graciously received, though not by the emperor in person. Instead, he was allowed to bow nine times to the emperor's empty throne. His presents were accepted. Most important of all, he was allowed to settle in the capital and was even given an annual allowance to pay for his living expenses. Now he could meet the most important officials of all. If he could convert them to Christianity, surely the ordinary, uneducated people would follow their example?

Respecting Chinese ways

The more Matteo Ricci learned about the Chinese, the more impressed he was. And what impressed him most was their peaceful attitude towards other countries. They were proud but not warlike:

It seems to be quite remarkable, when we stop to consider it, that in a kingdom of almost endless size, with more people than can be counted, and having plenty of everything, though they have a well-equipped army and navy that could conquer the neighbouring nations, neither the King nor his people ever think of fighting a war of conquest... In this respect they are much different from the people of Europe... While the nations of the West seem to be entirely taken up with the idea of power over others, they cannot even keep up what their ancestors have left them, as the Chinese have done for thousands of years.

■ How do you explain the Chinese attitude towards wars of conquest?

Ricci was very impressed by the strength of the Chinese attachment to tradition. Therefore he had to show that Christian beliefs did not go against the ideas of Confucius, the ancient philosopher whose rules governed Chinese society. The most important of these were ceremonies carried out by men to show respect for their ancestors. Ricci argued that this custom was not the same as worshipping them as gods. A Chinese could therefore become a Christian without neglecting his ancestors. Ricci's acceptance of Chinese tradition laid the foundations of the Catholic Church in China, and a number of educated Chinese became converts. When Ricci died, the emperor donated a piece of land for his grave, and the Mayor of Peking organised a large funeral procession and paid for a tombstone to honour his memory. It was engraved with these words:

Matteo Ricci with a Christian convert, Li Paulus, whose winged hat indicates his high rank

Together with Ricci, Li Paulus wrote Chinese translations of Latin astronomical works.

> To one who attained renown for justice and wrote famous books.

■ Can you think of a better epitaph for Ricci?

After Ricci, other Jesuits came to Peking and made themselves useful to the emperors of China. As technicians, they helped the Chinese cast their first cannon. As diplomats, they helped them negotiate their first treaty with a foreign power, Russia. By the eighteenth century about 300,000 Chinese had been converted to Christianity. But then the Jesuits' acceptance of ancestor ceremonies was attacked by other branches of the Catholic Church, such as the Dominicans and Franciscans. In 1745 the Pope upheld the views of the Dominicans and Franciscans against the Jesuits. The Chinese emperor replied by banning all Christian missionaries, and the Church in China went into a long decline.

1 What do you understand by the term 'civilised'? In what ways were the Chinese more civilised than the Europeans at this time?

2 Imagine that Ricci was able to use television, videos and other forms of mass media. How would he have used them to achieve his aims in China?

3 Why are good manners very important when you want to persuade someone to your point of view? Write some basic instructions on good behaviour and diplomacy for a newcomer to Britain today. What points would it have in common with what Ricci might have told a newcomer to China?

4 Compare the map on page 22 with a modern map of China and surrounding countries. How accurate is the seventeenth-century map?

Chinese exploration in the fifteenth century

Almost a century before Vasco da Gama (see page 8) crossed the Indian Ocean, a Chinese fleet did so under the command of Zheng He (1371–1433), a Muslim eunuch and soldier who had risen high in the service of the founders of the great Ming dynasty.

In 1405 Yung-Lo, the second Ming emperor, sent Zheng He into the 'Southern Ocean' at the head of sixty-two ships and 28,000 men. The expedition had two aims: to impress foreign rulers with the superiority of the Chinese; and to regulate trade so that the Chinese could pay for goods with their own favoured exports, such as silk and porcelain, rather than with gold and silver.

There were seven voyages in all. The first three went as far as India, the later ones on to the Persian Gulf, the Red Sea and the east coast of Africa. They visited at least fifty places previously unknown to the Chinese, bringing back tribute from many princes and also exotic animals such as ostriches, zebras and a giraffe. As a result of these voyages, ambassadors came to Peking from as far away as Bengal, Oman and east Africa.

These Chinese expeditions were very different from those of the Portuguese. They sought neither slaves nor plunder and wished neither to annex territory nor change people's religions.

But Zheng He's voyages were not popular in China. Courtiers jealous of his power said they were expensive and irrelevant to a land power like China. After Yung-Lo died in 1424 these criticisms grew and after Zheng He's death the voyages ceased. Official histories of the period ignored them altogether. No Henry the Navigator came to the throne of China, so Zheng He's brilliant exploits came to nothing.

William Adams

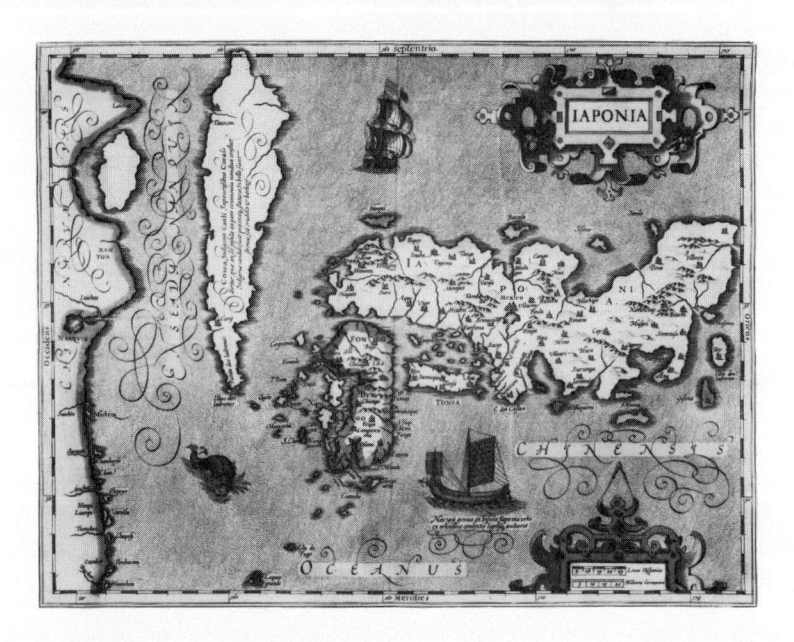

A seventeenth-century map of Japan

The English samurai

William Adams was an Englishman who helped the Dutch to take over the foreign trade of Japan for more than two hundred years. He was also the only foreigner who has ever been given the right to wear the two swords of a Japanese samurai (warrior).

Adams was born in Gillingham in Kent in 1564, the same year as Shakespeare was born. At the age of 12 he was apprenticed as a pilot on the Thames at Limehouse; then at 24 he was given command of his first ship, running supplies to the English fleet as it lay in wait for the Spanish Armada. For the next ten years he lived a life of high adventure, sailing southwards as far as the Barbary Coast in northern Africa and twice joining dangerous Dutch expeditions to find a 'north-east passage' around the frozen coasts of Russia to the Far East. No such passage was ever found; but Adams did become a fluent speaker of Dutch.

Voyage of disaster

In 1598 Adams was hired as the pilot of one of more than 20 Dutch ships setting out for the East. The voyage turned out to be a series of disasters. Leaving too late in the year to catch the most favourable winds, his fleet soon ran short of supplies. The men were so hungry that they stripped the leather covers off the ship's rigging and boiled them up to make soup. Then the fleet was split up by storms as it struggled past Cape Horn and into the Pacific. Left alone, the crew of Adams' ship, the *Liefde,* (which means 'charity' in Dutch) decided to make for Japan, which one of them had visited in 1585. They finally drifted ashore in April 1600. Of the 110 men who had sailed from Holland nearly two years before, only 24 were still alive and only six were well enough to work the ship.

■ Why do you think they decided to make for Japan?

The warlord

As the only senior officer fit enough to be interviewed, Adams was taken to meet a powerful warlord, Tokugawa Ieyasu. This is Adams' account of their meeting:

> the king demanded of me... what moved us to come to his land, being far off... (I said) that our land... desired friendship with all kings... in way of merchandise... Then he asked whether our country had wars? I answered him yea, with the Spaniards and Portuguese. He asked me in what did I believe? I said, in God, that made heaven and earth. He asked me *divers* other questions of things of my religion, and many other things – as what way we came to the country. Having a chart of the whole world, I showed him, through the Strait of Magellan. At which he wondered and thought me to lie. Thus, from one thing to another, I abode with him till midnight. And having asked me what merchandise we had in our ship I showed him all. In the end, he being ready to depart, I desired what we might have trade of merchandise, as the Portuguese and Spaniards had. To which he made me an answer, but what it was I did not understand. So he commanded me to be carried to prison.

various

1 Why do you think the warlord wanted to meet the stranger?
2 Why do you think Ieyasu asked the particular questions that he did?
3 What do you think of Adams' answers?

A man of influence

William Adams happened to arrive in Japan at a turning-point in its history. In October 1600 Ieyasu ended more than a century of civil wars in a decisive battle; this made him supreme warlord or *shogun,* able to rule the whole of the country in the name of the sacred emperor. He recognised Adams as a clever man with much useful knowledge, and ordered his release from prison. Adams soon became Ieyasu's trusted adviser on European technology and politics, and one of the most influential men in the kingdom. He taught the shogun about mathematics, gunnery and map-

Tokugawa Ieyasu

making and built him two ships of western design. He negotiated a trade treaty on the shogun's behalf with the Spanish-ruled Philippines. And he became so fluent in Japanese that he took the place of the Portuguese Jesuits as official interpreter at court. Ieyasu rewarded Adams with the rank of a samurai warrior, encouraged him to marry a Japanese lady and gave him an estate with 90 peasant families to work the land for him.

1 How did Adams' background prepare him for the position he attained?
2 Why do you think the shogun trusted him?

Two samurai warriors

A chance to go home

In 1609 a Dutch ship arrived in Japan. Trade with the West had until then been in the hands of the Portuguese and Spaniards, who were fellow Catholics and were ruled by the same king. Adams was delighted to see fellow Protestants and soon persuaded the shogun to give the Dutch the right to trade freely with the Japanese.

■ Why do you think the shogun agreed to give trading rights to the Dutch?

The Dutch found Adams very helpful indeed. He asked them to pass letters back to England so that his English wife and family could know that he was still alive and so that English merchants should come and join in the trade with Japan. But the Dutch simply tore his letters up without telling him.

■ Why do you think the Dutch treated Adams like this?

In 1613 an English ship, the *Clove,* finally arrived in Japan. By this time Adams' reputation was so great that English merchants already heard about him. Adams naturally helped his countrymen get the same trading rights as the Dutch. The captain of the *Clove* offered him a free passage back to England. The shogun had always forbidden Adams to leave Japan before; but now he said he could go. Adams had desperately wanted to see England for a long time; but he decided in the end not to go. Instead, he agreed to stay on and work for a trading company called the English East India Company as an adviser and pilot.

1 Why do you think the shogun finally agreed to let Adams go?
2 Why do you think Adams decided not to go?
3 How could Adams help the East India Company as an adviser?

A failure of enterprise

Adams turned out to be invaluable. Not only did he speak the language perfectly, he also knew what the Japanese most wanted to buy, how their systems of weights and measures worked, which officials had to be bribed and who could be trusted. Unfortunately, the English did not entirely trust Adams, whom they regarded as a 'naturalised Japanner'. They knew how absolutely they relied on him and that worried them. They did not like his closeness with the Japanese and they did not like his continuing friendship with the Dutch, his old friends and their great rivals. But they needed him and he continued to work for them until his death in 1620.

By then the fortunes of the English had turned very much for the worse. Only one of Adams' four voyages to Vietnam and Thailand on their behalf had shown a good profit. They had failed completely to get a share of the trade with China. Ieyasu had died in 1616 and his son did not like Adams or foreigners nearly as much as his father had. So the English lost most of their trading rights and were limited to a couple of small ports far from the capital. Richard Cocks, the head of the English trading station showed himself to be a well-meaning but incompetent leader, unable to stop his men from quarrelling and incapable even of keeping an orderly set of accounts. In 1623 he was summoned back to England to report to the directors of the East India Company, and the English trading station was closed down for good.

■ Which of the things that went wrong for the English would also have gone wrong for the Dutch?

Soon afterwards, the Spanish and Portuguese were expelled from Japan for fear that Christian Japanese might try to start another civil war against the Tokugawa family with outside Christian help. Only the Dutch were allowed to stay on. They promised to keep their religion to themselves and even loaned the shogun their ships and guns to help him crush a Christian rebellion. The Dutch had to live on a tiny island in Nagasaki harbour. But they kept a monopoly of Japanese trade until 1853, when the American navy arrived with modern gunboats and forced Japan to trade with other countries or face the possibility of bombardment.

1 Why do you think the Japanese were able to keep out Europeans for so long?

2 Write your own version of William Adams' first letter to his family back in England. Remember to include an account of his journey and details of his achievements during the past nine years. Include a picture of anything in the letter which you consider particularly interesting.

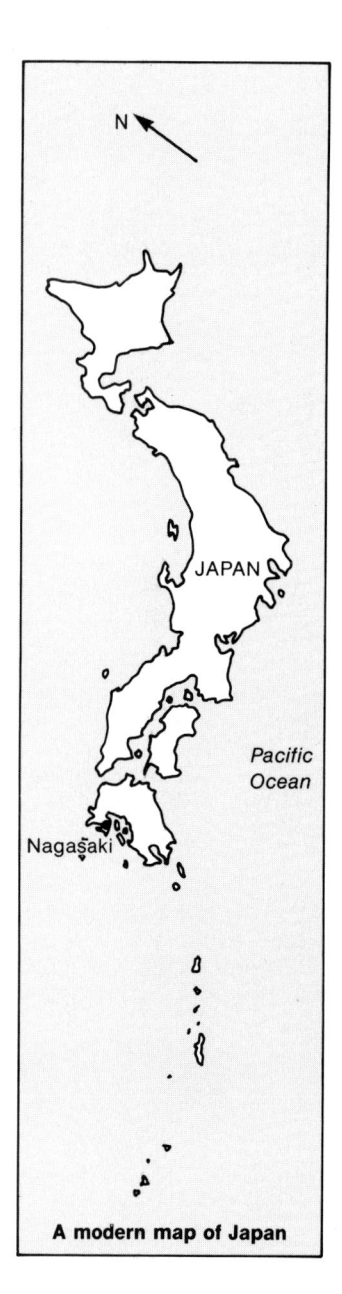

A modern map of Japan

Captain John Smith

Captain John Smith, 1580–1631

The lost colony

England's first attempt to found a colony in North America ended in disaster. No one knows for sure what happened to the settlers who were left on Roanoke Island, Virginia, in 1587. The next time a ship came to supply them, in 1590, they had simply disappeared. On a tree was carved the single word 'Croatoan', the name of another island.

■ What do you think might have happened to the settlers of Roanoke?

Jamestown

The first permanent English settlement in North America dates from 1607, but the survival of this colony too was very much in the balance for its first twenty years.

The expedition to colonise America was backed by the Virginia Company, a group of wealthy London merchants, who hoped the settlers would find gold and possibly a new trade route to India. In fact they found neither, and they wasted a great deal of time looking for them. Nor did the merchants who had invested money in the Virginia Company ever get anything back for it.

The settlers left England in December 1606 in three ships and sailed by way of the Canaries and the West Indies. Not until May 1607 did they land on the coast of Virginia, where they founded Jamestown, named in honour of their king, James I.

■ What problems do you think the settlers might have in colonising an unknown country?

Much of the settlers' food had spoiled on the long voyage. Hot weather and hard work soon took their toll, as this first-hand account by George Percy, one of the first settlers, makes clear:

> There were never Englishmen left in a foreign country in such misery as we were in this newly discovered Virginia. We *watched* every three nights, lying on the bare, cold ground ... and we stood guard all the next day, which brought our men to be most feeble wretches. Our food was but a small can of barley boiled in water for five men for a day; our drink was cold water taken out of the river, which was very salty at high tide and full of slime and filth at low tide, which was the destruction of many of our men. Thus we lived for the space of five months in this miserable distress, not having five able men to man our bulwarks upon any occasion.

kept watch

1 Why did the men have to stand guard all the time?
2 Why were food and water such a problem?

By September, 50 of the original 104 settlers had died. If friendly Indians had not brought them provisions, the rest might have died too. It was also fortunate for them that at this point Captain John Smith began to act as the leader of the colony.

Soldier of fortune

Smith had already had an exciting life by the time he joined the colonists bound for Virginia. At the age of 16 he had left home to become a soldier. He had fought in Austria against the Turks and on one occasion had taken on three Turkish champions in single combat, one after another, cutting the heads off each of them. When captured, he had been given as a slave to the wife of a Turkish commander, but had managed to escape and had finally made his way back to England.

It was this tough and resourceful adventurer who, by his energy, saved the dwindling colony, as another contemporary account makes clear:

THE INCONVENIENCIES

THAT HAVE HAPPENED TO SOME PERSONS WHICH HAVE TRANSPORTED THEMSELVES

from *England* to *Virginia*, without prouisions necessary to sustaine themselues, hath greatly hindred the *Progresse* of that noble *Plantation*: For preuention of the like disorders heereafter, that no man suffer, either through ignorance or misinformation; it is thought requisite to publish this short declaration: wherein is contained a particular of such necessaries, as either private families or single persons shall haue cause to furnish themselues with, for their better support at their first landing in Virginia: whereby also greater numbers may receiue in part, directions how to prouide themselues.

Apparrell.

		li.	s.	d.
	One Monmouth Cap	—	01	10
	Three falling bands	—	01	03
	Three shirts	—	07	06
	One waste-coate	—	02	02
	One suite of Canuase	—	07	06
	One suite of Frize	—	10	00
	One suite of Cloth	—	15	00
Apparrell for one man, and so after the rate for more.	Three paire of Irish stockins	—	04	—
	Foure paire of shoes	08	08	—
	One paire of garters	—	00	10
	One doozen of points	—	00	03
	One paire of Canuase sheets	—	08	00
	Seuen ells of Canuase, to make a bed and boulster, to be filled in *Virginia* 8. s.			
	One Rug for a bed 8. s. which with the bed seruing for two men, halfe is	}	08	00
	Fiue ells coorse Canuase, to make a bed at Sea for two men, to be filled with straw, iiij. s.	}	05	00
	One coorse Rug at Sea for two men, will cost vj. s. is for one			
		04	00	00

Victuall.

		li.	s.	d.
For a whole yeere for one man, and so for more after the rate.	Eight bushels of Meale	02	00	00
	Two bushels of pease at 3. s.	—	06	00
	Two bushels of Oatemeale 4. s. 6. d.	—	09	00
	One gallon of Aquauitæ	—	02	06
	One gallon of Oyle	—	03	06
	Two gallons of Vineger 1. s.	—	02	00
		03	03	00

Armes.

		li.	s.	d.
	One Armour compleat, light	—	17	00
For one man, but if halfe of your men haue armour it is sufficient so that all haue Peeces and swords.	One long Peece, fiue foot or fiue and a halfe, neere Musket bore	01	02	—
	One sword	—	05	—
	One belt	—	01	—
	One bandaleere	—	01	06
	Twenty pound of powder	—	18	00
	Sixty pound of shot or lead, Pistoll and Goose shot	—	05	00
		03	09	06

For a family of 6. persons and so after the rate for more.

Tooles.

	li.	s.	d.
Fiue broad howes at 2. s. a piece	—	10	—
Fiue narrow howes at 16. d. a piece	—	06	08
Two broad Axes at 3. s. 8. d. a piece	—	07	04
Fiue felling Axes at 18. d. a piece	—	07	06
Two steele hand sawes at 16. d. a piece	—	02	08
Two two-hand sawes at 5. s. a piece	—	10	—
One whip-saw, set and filed with box, file, and wrest	—	10	00
Two hammers 12. d. a piece	—	02	00
Three shouels 18. d. a piece	—	04	06
Two spades at 18. d. a piece	—	03	—
Two augers 6. d. a piece	—	01	00
Sixe chissels 6. d. a piece	—	03	00
Two percers stocked 4. d. a piece	—	00	08
Three gimlets 2. d. a piece	—	00	06
Two hatchets 21. d. a piece	—	03	06
Two froues to cleaue pale 18. d.	—	03	00
Two hand-bills 20. a piece	—	03	04
One grindlestone 4. s.	—	04	00
Nailes of all sorts to the value of	02	00	—
Two Pickaxes	—	03	—
	06	02	08

Houshold Implements.

	li.	s.	d.
One Iron Pot	—	07	—
One kettle	—	06	—
One large frying-pan	—	02	06
One gridiron	—	01	06
Two skillets	—	05	—
One spit	—	02	—
Platters, dishes, spoones of wood	—	04	—
	01	08	00

For a family of 6. persons, and so for more or lesse after the rate.

	li.	s.	d.
For Suger, Spice, and fruit, and at Sea for 6. men	—	12	06
So the full charge of Apparrell, Victuall, Armes, Tooles, and houshold stuffe, and after this rate for each person, will amount vnto about the summe of	12	10	—
The passage of each man is	06	00	—
The fraight of these prouisions for a man, will bee about halfe a Tun, which is	01	10	—
So the whole charge will amount to about	20	00	00

Nets, hookes, lines, and a tent must be added, if the number of people be greater, as also some kine.

And thus is the vsuall proportion that the Virginia *Company doe bestow vpon their Tenants which they send.*

Whosoeuer transports himselfe or any other at his owne charge vnto *Virginia*, shall for each person so transported before Midsummer 1625. haue to him and his heires for euer fifty Acres of Land vpon a first, and fifty Acres vpon a second diuision.

Imprinted at London by FELIX KYNGSTON. 1622.

The list of provisions was thought to be sufficient to sustain settlers on their arrival in Virginia.

Capt. Smith ... by his own example, good words and fair promises set some to mow, others to bind thatch, some to build houses, others to thatch them, himself always bearing the greatest task for his own share. In short time he provided most of them lodgings, neglecting any for himself. This done, seeing the savages great numbers begin to decrease, (he) ... shipped himself in the *shallop* to search the country for trade ... He went down the river to *Keoughtan* where at first they scorned him as a starved man, yet he so dealt with them that the next day they loaded his boat with corn.

small boat
an Indian village

Smith's method of 'dealing' with the Indians had been to get his men to fire off their guns.

1 Why did Smith think it so important to build proper shelters?

2 Why do you think the Indians decided to give some provisions to Smith?

Pocahontas

Later that first winter, Smith went out scouting for more food, only to be captured by Indians. This is what he said happened to him:

At *his* [Smith's] entrance before the king, all the people gave a great shout ... Having feasted him after their best barbarous manner they could, a long consultation was held ... two great stones were brought before *Powhaten* [the Indian chief]. Then as many as could laid hands on him, dragged him to them, and thereon laid his head, and being ready with their clubs to beat out his brains, Pocahontas, the king's dearest daughter, when no entreaty could prevail, got his head in her arms and laid her own upon his to save him from death; whereat the emperor was contented he should live.

John Smith capturing an Indian King

John Smith's life is saved by Pocahontas.

This incident makes a dramatic story and became very famous. But is it true? When he first wrote about his capture a few months after they released him, Smith makes no mention of Pocahontas at all. The account quoted on the previous page is taken from the *History of Virginia*, written much later and after Pocahontas herself had become famous by marrying John Rolfe, one of the Jamestown settlers, and visiting England with him. The whole story rests on Smith's word alone and he had quite a reputation for tall tales, but whenever historians have been able to check what he said about his adventures in Turkey or America they have found them to be pretty well true.

Whatever the truth of the Pocahontas incident, she certainly became the guardian angel of the colony, as Smith himself made clear:

> Had the savages not fed us, we directly had starved. And this relief... was commonly brought us by this Lady Pocahontas... when inconstant fortune turned our peace to war, this tender virgin would still... dare to visit us... and during the time of two or three years she next under God was still the instrument to preserve this colony from death, famine and utter confusion.

1 Do you think Smith could have lied and got away with it? (Remember Pocahontas knew the truth.)

2 Why was Pocahontas able to help the settlers? Why do you think she did?

Propaganda for the colony

After these years of hardship Smith himself was injured in an accident and so returned to England in 1609. He never went back to Jamestown but he did publish a detailed account of the new colony in a pamphlet called *A Map of Virginia*. He described the Indians as 'very strong, of an able body and full of agility' but also as untrustworthy and 'covetous of copper, beads and such like trash'. He also described their magnificent clothes of painted deerskins and turkey feathers, their elaborate tattoos and fantastic adornments:

In each ear commonly they have three great holes, whereat they hang chains, bracelets or copper. Some of their men wear in those holes a small green and yellow coloured snake, near half a yard in length... Others wear a dead rat tied by the tail. Some of their heads wear the wing of a bird or some large feather with a rattle... Their heads and shoulders are painted red.

Smith also made it clear that Indian men and women lived very different lives:

The men bestow their time in fishing, hunting wars and such man-like exercises ... Which is the cause that the women be very *painful* [busy] and the men often idle. The women and children do the rest of the work. They make mats, baskets, pots, *pound* [grind] their corn, make their bread ... bear all kinds of burdens.

■ Smith's pamphlet makes Virginia out to be a very interesting place. But he makes no mention of the hardships of living there. Why do you think this was?

A watercolour, c1590, of an Indian settlement in Virginia

The colony survives

Thanks to John Rolfe, the man who married Pocahontas, the settlers at last found a way to make a living – by growing tobacco. The death-rate however still remained appallingly high. By 1616, of the 1,600 people who had gone out to Virginia, only 350 remained alive. By 1624 there were 1,200 out of a total of 6,000. No wonder Smith had called it in one of his letters 'a misery, a ruin, a death, a hell'.

■ Why do you think the death-rate remained so high?

Return to the New World

John Smith returned to the coast of North America in 1614, sailing on behalf of another group of London merchants, who were still hoping to find gold and copper mines, just as the Spanish had in South America. Smith brought back fish and furs instead, which were to become important items of trade over the next two centuries. He also made a map from which the name New England was given to the region he had visited.

Smith probably knew more about America than any other Englishman of his day, but he also knew how much more there was to know:

A map of New England by John Smith

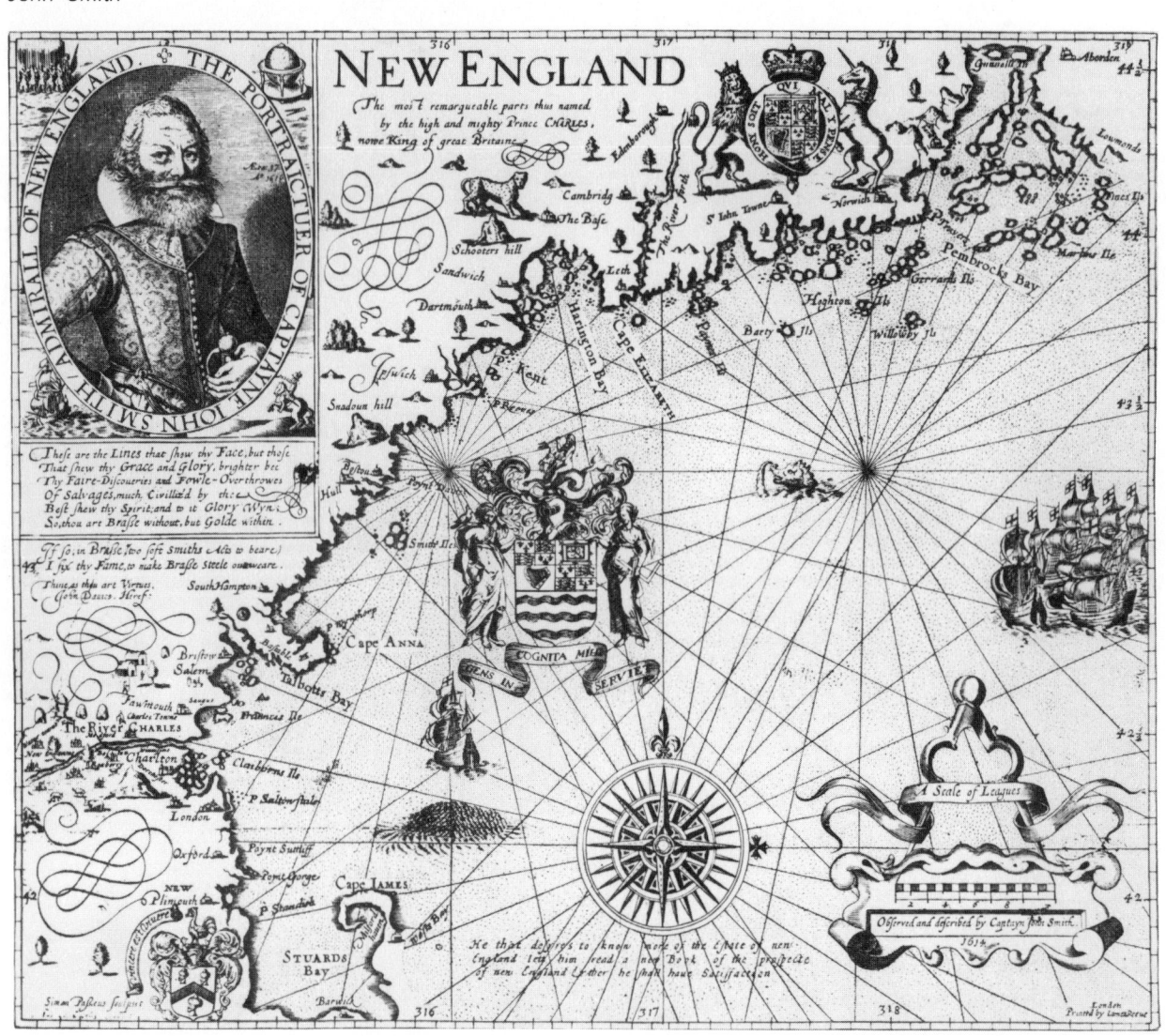

As for the goodness and fine substance of the land, we are for the most part altogether ignorant of them, but only here and there where we have touched or seen a little, the edges of these large dominions which do stretch themselves into the main, God doth know how many thousand miles.

1 Why do you think it was to take a very long time to get an accurate idea of the geography of North America?

2 Suppose that Pocahontas had written a history of Virginia. What might she have said about a) John Smith; b) the English colonists.

3 Design an advertisement to encourage settlers to come to Virginia. You must decide whether your advertisement will be biased, showing only the favourable side of life out there, or whether you will warn people in advance of the dangers that could be encountered, and stressing the qualities which are needed for survival.

4 Write a conversation between two Indians who disagree about whether to welcome English settlers or to attack them. Draw a picture illustrating the argument of one of them.

5 Find out which of the present-day states of the USA form New England.

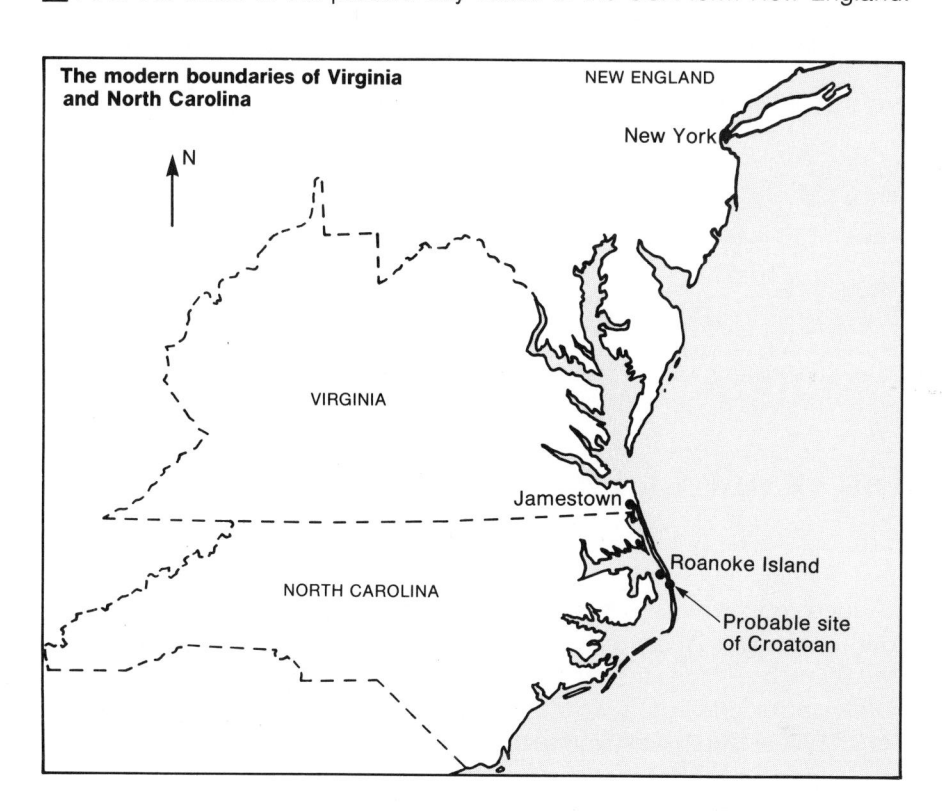

The modern boundaries of Virginia and North Carolina

Jan Huyghen van Linschoten

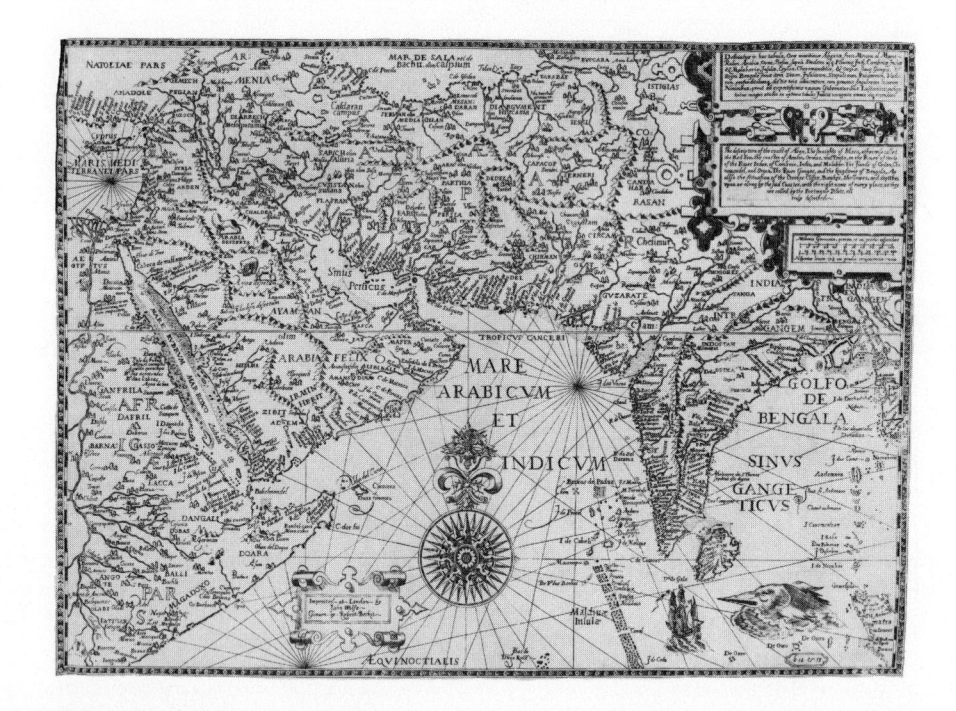

A sixteenth-century map of the Indian Ocean

This map appears in Linschoten's 'Itinerario'.

The revolt of the Netherlands

In the mid-sixteenth century the Netherlands was a small province of the great empire ruled by the Habsburg Charles V. (The Habsburg empire included most of what is now Germany, Spain, Italy, Hungary and much of South America.) A century later the Netherlands was an independent country with a worldwide empire of its own. The key to these changes was Dutch command of the sea, as this petition to the Emperor from the States-General (the Dutch Parliament) in 1548 makes clear:

> the province of Holland is a very small country ... almost enclosed by the sea on three sides ... Moreover, the said province ... contains many dunes, bogs and lakes ... unfit for crops or pasture ... Consequently, the main business of the country must be in shipping ... from which a great many people earn their living.

■ What sort of people could earn their living directly or indirectly from shipping and trade?

The Dutch struggle for independence began after Philip II succeeded his father, Charles V. As a devout Catholic, he believed he had a duty to stamp out Protestantism. The Dutch rose against him in 1566, and it took them over thirty years to drive out the Spanish forces. Dutch independence was finally recognised in 1648.

The key to the East

Supported by Elizabeth of England, the Dutch used their big shipping fleet to attack Spanish shipping. In 1580 Philip II took over Portugal and stopped the Portuguese from selling to the Dutch the spices they had brought over from the East. So the Dutch decided to go direct to the East Indies for their spices. The problem was how to get there?

The Portuguese had opened up the direct sea route to the East almost a century before. But they kept it a closely guarded secret. In 1504 King Manuel had forbidden any published map to show the route to the East beyond the mouth of the River Congo in Africa.

The man who gave the Dutch the key to the East was Jan Huyghen van Linschoten. For seven years he had worked as a servant for a Portuguese archbishop in India. When he came back to Holland, Linschoten wrote a world geography which included a detailed description of the route from Lisbon to Goa in southern India. This was published in 1595 as a book called *Itinerario*. Using Linschoten's book, four Dutch ships under the command of Cornelis de Houtman sailed to Java and back. The voyage took two and a half years and cost the lives of 200 out of 289 men, but it made a profit and proved that the Portuguese could not hold the door closed against rivals. The race to the East was on.

■ Why were the Dutch prepared to go to such extraordinary lengths to break into the spice trade of the East?

Jan Huyghen van Linschoten

An empire in the East

In 1598, 22 ships left Holland for the East. Most of the 13 who went via the Cape of Good Hope came back loaded with paper and nutmeg. Nine went via the Strait of Magellan (including William Adams's *Liefde* – see page 28). One of these, commanded by Oliver van Noort, became the first Dutch ship to sail right round the world.

In 1602 the States-General persuaded the merchants who had financed voyages to the East to join up and form the United Dutch East India Company (VOC – Vereenigde Oost-Indische Compagnie). The English East India Company had been set up in 1600; but the VOC had ten times as much money backing it. The VOC was given a monopoly of all trade between the Cape of Good Hope and the Strait of Magellan. It also had powers that normally only governments have – to coin money, to raise armies and to make peace and war.

A portrait of a prosperous Dutch trader and his wife who lived near the port of Batavia (now Jakarta, Indonesia)

1 Imagine you are a member of the States-General. Write a speech to persuade merchants to join the VOC.

The most important creator of the Dutch eastern empire was Jan Pieterszoon Coen, who set up trading posts at Batavia (near Jakarta in Java) and in Formosa (Taiwan). In 1641 the Dutch took Malacca from the Portuguese and in 1658 forced them out of Ceylon (Sri Lanka) as well. Thanks to the Englishman William Adams, they also gained control of the trade of Japan. Around 1700 the VOC brought coffee plants from Arabia to Java. Coffee soon became a fabulous new eastern export, growing from 100 pounds (approximately 45.5 kilograms) in 1711 to 12,000,000 (almost 5.5 metric tonnes) in 1723.

2 Imagine you are a Dutch merchant living in the East. Write a letter to your brother to persuade him to send his son to join you in the East. Remember that he may have some worries about this.

3 Coffee was a completely new product for Europeans around the turn of the seventeenth century. Prepare an advertisement promoting coffee amongst the Europeans, for presentation either in written or printed form or by you personally. How are you going to persuade a potential European consumer to buy it or at least try it?

The Americas

Like the English, the Dutch tried to find a new route to the East via the northern coast of Russia. Three voyages in the 1590s failed. In 1609 the VOC hired Henry Hudson, an Englishman, to try again. He mistakenly went north-west instead, discovering the area now known as New York and sailing up the Hudson River. Dutch interest in northern waters did lead to control of the whaling industry and profitable trade with Russia and the Baltic in furs and 'naval stores' (timber, tar, hemp and flax).

■ Why were 'naval stores' important goods for countries like Holland and England?

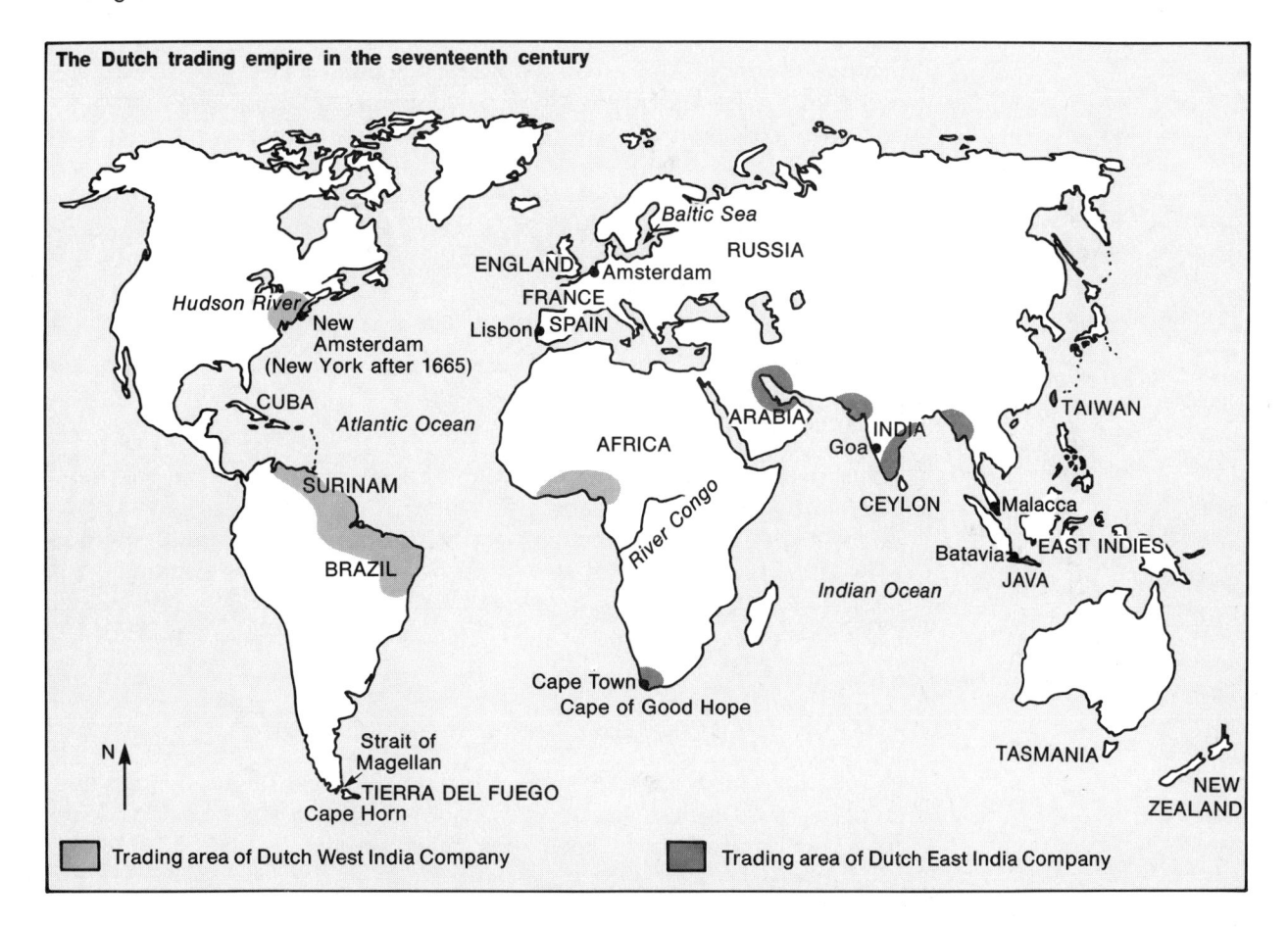

The Dutch trading empire in the seventeenth century

[Map showing the Dutch trading empire with labels: Hudson River, New Amsterdam (New York after 1665), Cuba, Atlantic Ocean, Surinam, Brazil, Strait of Magellan, Tierra del Fuego, Cape Horn, Baltic Sea, England, Amsterdam, France, Lisbon, Spain, Russia, Africa, River Congo, Cape Town, Cape of Good Hope, Arabia, Goa, India, Ceylon, Malacca, Batavia, East Indies, Java, Indian Ocean, Taiwan, Tasmania, New Zealand. Legend: Trading area of Dutch West India Company; Trading area of Dutch East India Company]

In 1621 the Dutch set up a West India Company to trade with the New World and west Africa. As Holland was still fighting Spain intermittently, this meant, in practice, attacking Spanish and Portuguese ships and poaching in the profitable slave trade. In 1628 the Dutch captured the entire Spanish treasure fleet off Cuba; but capturing treasure fleets can never make reliable profits, as a regular business can. The Dutch West India Company followed up Hudson's voyages and settled 'New Amsterdam' (now New York); but most of its efforts went into trying to gain control of Brazil. The Portuguese finally drove out the Dutch from Brazil in 1654, but the Dutch did hold on to Surinam (Dutch Guiana). In 1664 the English took over the Dutch colony along the Hudson, but the Dutch held on to their share in the growing Atlantic trade in slaves and sugar.

■ Why were the Dutch more interested in Brazil than New York?

The Pacific

Isaac Le Maire, a Dutch merchant from Hoorn, wanted to break the VOC monopoly by finding a new route to the East. In 1616 he sent Willem Schouten with two ships to find a way. They passed the Strait of Magellan and rounded Tierra del Fuego, which everyone had thought was part of an unknown continent named Terra Australis. Schouten proved it was an island and called its southern-most point Cape Hoorn, after his home port. When he finally reached the East Indies he was arrested, but a court in Holland proved he had found a new route, and the VOC had to return his ship to him and pay damages.

1 What does this episode show you about Dutch attitudes to trade?

2 Prepare a concise statement, with a supporting map or diagram, for Willem Schouten to take into court to prove that he had found a new route to the East Indies.

Many ships blundered onto the barren coasts of Australia but the most careful attempt at exploration was made by Abel Tasman in 1642. He discovered Tasmania – although he did not know it was an island – and New Zealand, which he thought was the coast of a large continent. His discoveries had no value for trade, so it was left to the English sailor Captain Cook to complete Tasman's work of discovery a century later.

Africa

In 1652 the Dutch founded Cape Town on the Cape of Good Hope as a stopping-place on the way to the East, where Dutch ships could pick up fresh food and water to keep their crews healthy.

■ Why was this settlement so important in the long run?

Greatness and decline

Between 1585 and 1622 the population of Amsterdam grew from 30,000 to 105,000. Immigrants came from France and Germany looking for work. Some were refugees. Religious freedom allowed Catholics, Protestants and

Jews to live and work together peacefully. By 1660 the population had reached 200,000, and one third was foreign by birth or parentage. Amsterdam had become a world centre for shipping and trade, with banks and insurance companies, massive warehouses and a complex system of canals. The city also made its living by processing imported goods, such as silk, leather, wool and sugar, into finished goods, and skilled craftsmen made Amsterdam famous for its books, maps, guns, lenses, gemstones and paintings.

■ How can you tell that there were many rich people in Amsterdam?

In 1672 the English consul, Sir William Temple, published his *Observations Upon the United Provinces of the Netherlands* and noted:

> The old severe and frugal way of living is now almost quite out of date in Holland... Instead of convenient dwellings, the Hollanders now build stately palaces, have their delightful gardens... keep coaches. No apparel can serve them but the best and richest that France and other countries afford; and their sons are so much addicted to *play* [gambling] that many families are quite ruined by it.

A panorama of Amsterdam, a city built on overseas trade, in 1575

Notice how ships could sail right into the city centre.

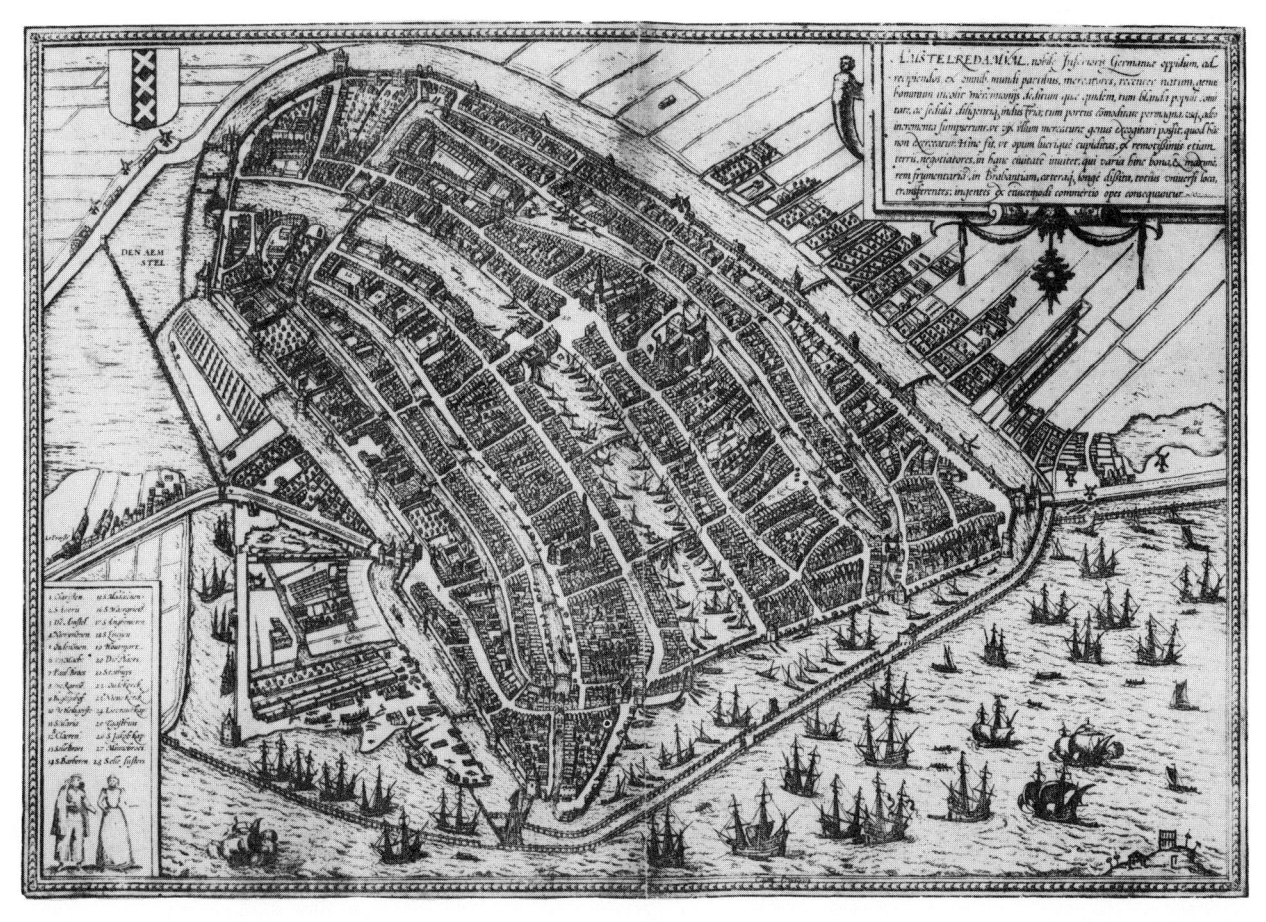

1 Why do you think Holland had begun to change like this?

2 What effects do you think these changes would have on their empire?

Holland had become a very comfortable place to live in. Perhaps too comfortable. Much of her wealth and strength had been spent in ventures that had been unsuccessful or in wars against Spain, England and France – all bigger countries. Life in Holland was to remain comfortable; but her great neighbours were to take over as the leaders in empire and commerce.

3 Which Dutch ventures had not paid off? Which had?

Europe and the world in 1700

A map of the world, c1690

By 1700, European merchants, missionaries and settlers had founded new communities in every part of the world except Australia and the polar regions. None of these settlements was strong enough to survive without the support of the countries which had created them. Without the men, goods and guns which were sent there and the produce which was sent back home, these trading posts, forts and plantations would soon have been abandoned by their inhabitants or taken over by local peoples. But they were supported and grew to become thriving colonies which centuries later were to become independent nations.

The pattern of European settlement varied greatly. Along the eastern coasts of North America, English and French settlers pushed inland, against the often violent but unsuccessful resistance of native Americans, who were unable to unite amongst themselves. Further south and in the Caribbean the white settlers formed a planter aristocracy, supported by the labour of black slaves brought from Africa under horrendous conditions to work on plantations growing sugar, tobacco, rice, indigo and, later, cotton, for export to northern Europe, where these crops could not be grown.

In South America, the Spanish and Portuguese were divided between *peninsulares* (those born in Spain) and *criollos* (who were locally born). The peninsulares were given most of the top jobs in church and government, but they were united with the criollos at least in their desire to profit from the fabulous mineral wealth of the continent and in their efforts to push the frontier of Indian resistance even further into the interior. By 1700 they had created cities, cathedrals and universities which could rival those of Europe in magnificence and far outshone the achievements of their fellow Europeans further north.

European penetration of Africa was far more limited, though there was a booming trade along its western coast, where guns, cloth and metal goods made in Europe were exchanged for slaves, gold and ivory from the interior. Climate and disease, however, prevented Europeans settling in significant numbers.

Disease remained a major risk for Europeans migrating anywhere. Between 1604 and 1634 no less than 25,000 soldiers died in the Royal Hospital at Goa (India), most of them shortly after their arrival. And of the 329 Jesuits known to have left Lisbon for China between 1581 and 1721 at least 127 died at sea, most before even reaching Goa.

In Asia, the Europeans were still far less powerful than the rulers of the lands whose wealth they had came to tap. Their tactics had changed now from piracy to diplomacy. In the old days fortunes had been made on single voyages when spices, silks and jewels could be sold at an immense profit in Europe. These goods were still valued and provided a profitable trade. But by the eighteenth century Europe's growing middle classes offered a great new market for bulkier products like tea, coffee, porcelain and cotton goods. Trading on this scale demanded order and security.

While the expansion of commerce changed the lives of Europeans and the peoples they traded with, the desire of Europeans to spread the Christian religion seemed to slacken. This reflects partly a weakening of the Catholic church, partly the indifference of the increasingly active Protestant powers to the conversion of the natives, and partly the stout resistance of Muslims,

Hindus and Buddhists to alien ideas. Missionary work did still go on but its successes were isolated and piecemeal compared with the rapid spiritual conquest of South America in the sixteenth century.

The technical and military superiority of Europeans over other peoples was, however, far from slackening. Their ships were getting ever more efficient, their navigation more accurate and their guns more devastating. Power brought confidence and also greed and cruelty, as the Europeans struggled to dominate non-Europeans where they could and to shut out rival Europeans where they could not. An age of encounters was giving way to an age of empires.

■ Draw a time chart to show the main voyages and events that you have read about.

Find out more for yourself

1. Imagine you have a chance to organise a tour tracing the footsteps of one of the people in this book. Which one will you choose? What methods of travel would you use? Draw a map showing the places you would visit.

2. Some of the people in this book are well-known in other countries. You could write to a school in the USA and find out what they teach about Captain John Smith. Or you could write to Japan and ask about William Adams. In Japan they call him Miura Anjin. You can write in English (clearly!) because everyone over 12 in Japan has to learn English at school.

3. Which of the people in this book would you most like to meet and why? You could write an imaginary interview between yourself and your favourite person and then tape record it.

4. One result of increased contact between Europeans and other peoples was to introduce new words into European languages like English. From North America came many new words for different kinds of plants and animals that are only found there. From India came words such as pyjama, shampoo, dinghy, gingham and bungalow. See what other words you can find that have come into English from Asia, Africa or America.

5. Devise a game based on the theme of travel, trade or exploration. It could be a computer game or a board game on the lines of snakes and ladders with lots of hazards like storms and deserts. Look through the book again for ideas.

6. The following books will tell you more about South America, and you may find others in your library:

    R Tames, *The Conquest of South America* (Methuen, 1971)
    B R Lewis, *Growing Up in Aztec Times* (Batsford, 1981)
    B R Lewis, *Growing Up in Inca Times* (Batsford, 1981)

Index

Africa   1, 2, 6, 7, 8, 16-21, 43
America, North   32-9, 43
   South   10-15, 38, 48
Amsterdam   44-5
Aristotle   12
astronomy   24

Barbary Coast   3, 19, 28

Cameos, Luis de   9
Charles V   40-1
China   2, 9, 22-7
Christianity   11-14, 23, 25
Columbus, Christopher   4, 8, 11
Confucius   26
coffee   42

Death-rates   15, 48
Dias, Bartolomeo   8
Dominicans   13
Dutch   28-31, 40-6

East India Company   30-1

Gama, Vasco da   8
Goa   41, 48

Herodotus   21
Hudson, Henry   43

Japan   1, 2, 28-31
Jesuits   26, 48

Leo of Rozmital   5
Leo X   16-17
Lisbon   5, 8

Manuel of Portugal   8, 9
maps   2, 24, 29, 38, 41

New England, 38-9
Niger   21

Park, Mungo   21
Peking   22, 25, 26
Philip II   13, 41
Pocahontas   35-6, 39
Portugal   5-9

Roanoke colony   2, 32
Rolfe, John   36-7

Schouten, Willem   44
Sepulveda   12, 13
slavery   6, 7, 8, 11-14, 18, 20
Songhay   18-20
Spain   10-15, 17, 40-1
spices   41
sugar   7, 44

Tasman, Abel   44
tea   4
Timbuktu   18-19
tobacco   4, 37
Tokugawa Ieyasu   29-30

Virginia   32-7

White, John   2

Zheng He   27

Acknowledgements

The author and publishers are grateful to the following for permission to reproduce material:

Bibliothèque Nationale, Paris, page 3; Bild-Archiv der Österreichischen Nationalbibliotek, Wien, pages 6 and 45; The British Library, pages 12, 13, 16, 22 and 40; The Trustees of the British Museum, page 37; Cambridge University Press, page 15; Chatsworth Settlement Trustees and the Courtauld Institute of Art, page 17; John Carter Brown Library at Brown University, USA, page 34; The Lilly Library, Indiana University, USA, page 25; Mary Evans Picture Library, pages 6 and 21; National Maritime Museum, pages 4, 10, 11, 28, 38 and 47; Rijksmuseum, Amsterdam, pages 41 and 42; School of Oriental and African Studies, University of London, page 30; South American Pictures, page 12; Virginia State Library, Virginia, USA, pages 32, 35 and 36.

The picture on the front cover is a detail from *Ships trading in the East*, painted by Hendrik Cornelis Vroom (1566-1640), reproduced with the permission of the Trustees of the National Maritime Museum.

Every effort has been made to contact copyright holders, but we apologise if any have been overlooked.

A World of Change

This book is part of a series entitled *A World of Change*, intended for the 11-14 age group. The aim of the whole series is to combine a firm framework of historical fact with a 'skill-based' approach. The factual content provides continuity, and the opportunity to study causation and development. It is balanced by the two other vital ingredients for lively study of history: opportunity for 'empathy', which enables children to make an imaginative leap into the past; and study of a variety of original sources, both written and visual.

The series comprises a core textbook which studies a number of themes important in the Early Modern Age, approximately 1450-1700; a number of linked topic books; and a teacher's book for the whole series (which includes copyright-free worksheets).

The core book is primarily concerned with the British Isles, but within the context of what was happening in the rest of the world, known and unknown. The well-known political, religious and economic themes are considered. So too are the lives of ordinary men, women and children, and the way in which both change and continuity affected them. The book does not set out to be a full chronological survey, but it is hoped that it is sufficiently flexible to be used in that way if desired.

The core textbook is complete in itself, but has also been designed to provide a number of stepping-off points for 'patch studies'. Opportunities for this kind of work are provided by the eight *World of Change* topic books which are clearly linked to the themes in the main book. However, the topic books are also designed so that they can be used on their own if desired. All the topic books are listed on the back cover.

For the teacher

The theme of culture contact can be linked to many other curricular areas such as geography (maps and navigation), RE (missionaries and other religions), as well as art (paintings of the exotic), maths (astronomy), biology (movements of diseases, plants and animals), and language (loan words). The bibliography for this subject area is vast but heavily weighted towards a European viewpoint. One obviously needs to watch this, trying to ensure that non-European viewpoints are represented adequately.

Detailed suggestions for further reading are given in the Teacher's Book which accompanies this series. Outstanding writers include C Cipolla (on technological aspects), J H Parry (for broad narrative), C R Boxer (on the Portuguese and Dutch especially), and F Braudel who has the rare ability to present both a masterly overview and fascinating scraps of detail.

© Richard Tames 1987

All rights reserved. No part of this publication may be reproduced, stored in a retrieval system or transmitted in any form or by any means, electronic, mechanical, photocopying, recording or otherwise, without the prior written consent of the copyright holders. Applications for such permission should be addressed to the publishers: Stanley Thornes (Publishers) Ltd, Old Station Drive, Leckhampton, CHELTENHAM GL53 0DN, England.

First published in 1987 by:
Stanley Thornes (Publishers) Ltd
Old Station Drive
Leckhampton
CHELTENHAM GL53 0DN
England

Typeset by Tech-Set, Gateshead, Tyne & Wear
Printed and bound in Great Britain by
Ebenezer Baylis & Son Ltd, Worcester

British Library Cataloguing in Publication Data

Tames, Richard
   Exploring other civilizations.—(World
   of change topic books)
   1. Civilization—History
   I. Title   II. Series
   909'.5   CB69

ISBN 0-85950-547-2